MEN: A USER'S GUIDE

MEN:
A USER'S
GUIDE

(From toilet training to bedtime battles)

Kathy Lette

BANTAM PRESS

LONDON • TORONTO • SYDNEY • AUCKLAND • JOHANNESBURG

TRANSWORLD PUBLISHERS
61–63 Uxbridge Road, London W5 5SA
A Random House Group Company
www.rbooks.co.uk

First published in Great Britain
in 2010 by Bantam Press
an imprint of Transworld Publishers

A CIP catalogue record for this book
is available from the British Library.

ISBN 9780593060117

Addresses for Random House Group Ltd companies outside the UK
can be found at: www.randomhouse.co.uk
The Random House Group Ltd Reg. No. 954009

The Random House Group Limited supports The Forest Stewardship
Council (FSC), the leading international forest-certification organization.
All our titles that are printed on Greenpeace-approved FSC-certified paper carry
the FSC logo. Our paper procurement policy can be found at
www.rbooks.co.uk/environment

Typeset in 11/15pt Berkeley Book by
Falcon Oast Graphic Art Ltd.
Printed and bound in Great Britain by
Clays Ltd, Bungay, Suffolk

2 4 6 8 10 9 7 5 3 1

This book is dedicated to the comedic coven, otherwise known as my mum, Val, daughter Georgie and my three sisters, Jenny, Liz and Cara. And to all my Aussie girlfriends, especially 'The Gerts' (our home is girt by sea), Catherine Dovey, Jean Kittson, Alison Magney, Susie Carleton, Angela Bowne, Jenny Bott, Emily Booker and Shaz Allan.

Contents

Introduction

God, apparently as a prank, devised two sexes and called them 'opposite'. The sex war has raged for 5,000 years. But surely it's time we called a truce ... starting with men negotiating their terms of surrender.

Why do men like intelligent women? Because opposites attract. Just look at the evidence. What excites most men? Food, footy, a beer and the Playboy channel. The trouble is, women get all excited about nothing ... and then we marry him.

Men are just like those gadgets you buy which read 'A little assembly required' – then sit in the corner all in pieces for centuries. If only blokes came with some operating instructions.

With regard to the male of the species, I often feel like a zoologist who has dropped in on a bunch of gorillas and forgotten my tranquillizer gun. How much easier if men were given descriptive names, as in ye olden times, like Attila the Hun and Ivan the Terrible. Cheating Ratbag Misogynist the Third would so take the guesswork out of dating.

We women need a user's guide. Having dedicated myself to years of in-depth research into the subject of men (I'm named after a diary and I've had many entries), and with a Ph.D. in the glaringly obvious, in this owner's manual I offer you my top tips on how to understand, house-train, tame and, in extreme cases, bump off your bloke.

P.S. I do all my research in the most scientific fashion – over cappuccinos with girlfriends. (Well, a writer can't have all work and no plagiarism!) But if I've given away any secrets please address your complaints to my *nom de plume* – Miss Quote.

CHAPTER 1

Dating

There are many good things about being female.

1) You get off sinking ships first.

2) You don't have to readjust genitalia in public.

3) You can scare male bosses, policemen or aged judges with mysterious gynaecological disorders or the mere mention of the word 'tampon'.

The only bad thing is that there is only one other sex available to us.

Dating means gambling with fate and losing so many times that a girl gets roulette rash. Men problems: now *there's* a tautology. But you can't stay cooped up inside all the time on your own. I mean, the Home Shopping Channel operator is starting to recognize your voice.

One thing's for sure, whether you crave a toyboy or an old guy who is really rich and quite ill . . . when it comes to men you may be a shopaholic, but you're bound to end up with a bloke you hadn't bargained on.

Types of date

Internet dating   Best not to rely on the kindness of passing serial killers. Internet dating turns you into a marital limbo dancer – your expectations just keep getting lower and lower until you're scraping the bottom of the biological barrel.

Blind dates   I've been on so many blind dates I should be given a free dog. Love may be blind, but dates should not be. By the entrée you'll have discovered that you're completely incompatible. Your rising sign is Aquarius . . . and he's a complete bastard. (Tell him your sign is 'Do Not Disturb'.)

Office sex   Even though there is a man shortage, never resort to your boss. He'll be married, of course. This is called sleeping your way to the bottom. There's only one reason a man sleeps with his secretary: he just loves a woman he can dictate to.

So what kind of man should you have on your menu?

Toyboys

Pros of toyboy dating

Birthdays are nature's way of telling a woman to get a toyboy.

*

No woman is ever old enough to know better.

*

Date a toyboy and the tube announcement 'Mind the gap' will take on a whole new meaning. But let's look at the biological facts. The male of the species hits his sexual prime in his late teens; a woman in her late forties. You don't have to be Einstein to do the maths. I mean, 19 goes into 50 a hell of a lot more than 50 goes into 19. A toyboy's vocabulary may be small, but who cares when he ends every sentence with a proposition?

*

I once dated a boy ten years younger than me and only lab rabbits had more sex than us. We had phone sex – but in the booth. We did it while listening to music – but in the back row of the concert hall. His headboard should have come with an airbag. I was an FBI agent's dream – I had fingerprints all over me.

*

Why can't women grow old disgracefully? Just think, somewhere right now Berlusconi's next lover is being potty-trained.

*

But just as fashionable clothes date one so quickly, so do some dates. I mean what is Madonna going to do with Jesus? Date him or adopt him?

*

While older male intellectuals have the motor skills of a rust-riddled Lada, a toyboy's every sperm droplet could be entered individually in a rodeo. The trouble is, he may have a strong libido but can he spell it? He probably thinks it means the words in an opera. Although 'opera' isn't exactly in his vocabulary either. Except next to the word 'soap'.

*

A part of you knows that sex with a toyboy is an illusion, a sexual chimera. But the other part of your brain scoffs at that notion. It isn't a mirage . . . It just looks like one.

*

You'll get lots of caustic cracks about why you didn't childproof your love life. You'll jokingly be told to make sure you buy him a booster seat for the car . . . But in truth, age doesn't matter – not unless you're a building or a Stilton or a grapevine.

*

The guy may not have any higher education but he has *heaps* of lower. (Think Rent-a-Bulge.)

You'll be the envy of all. When eyeing those taut, brown buns in those skimpy bathers – we're talking the kind of pneumatic buttocks that have done more for female masturbation than Dr Ruth – every woman in a ten-mile radius will prepare to leave her partner pronto and have his love-child, as she watches him caress his chiselled abs with sunscreen Factor Lust.

*

Even though men regularly leave their wives for teenagers, it's still a scandal for an older woman to take a toy. But don't worry. Just because you're running around with a man old enough to be your son doesn't mean your friends are sniggering behind your back . . . They're *guffawing*. Out loud. To your face. If they ask you with disdain, 'Where's your self-respect?' just reply, 'I don't know. My toyboy's the one who puts everything away.'

*

An ad for a toyboy: 'Must adore me, not bore me and do all my chores for me.'

Cons of toyboy dating

Maybe you're having an early menopause? And he's your hot flush?

*

When you told him you wanted him to show more interest in your family, you didn't mean date your daughter.

*

If there's one thing the Nouveau Poor need, it's a niche with the Nouveau Riche. A wealthy older woman fits the bill, literally.

*

Toyboys are so broke, he's probably only marrying you for the rice.

*

A fool and her money are soon married. And in you he's found a wife he can really bank on. After all, you're a woman with money to burn. In a toyboy you may have met your match.

*

Toyboys live on a shoestring – a Gucci shoestring.

*

'Do you take this woman to the cleaners, for 50 per cent of her income, from this day forth, for richer and richer?'

'You bloody well bet I do!'

'I now pronounce you man and mansion.'

*

A wealthy wife is quite a labour-saving device. Make him sign a pre-nuptial agreement you could make into a mini-series.

*

You'll have so much in common with your toyboy. You have a Caribbean island, and he wants one . . .

*

You'll feel like a teenager ... but is that a good look on a woman who is contemplating her first incontinence pad?

*

You'll have to spend all your waking hours reversing out of rooms so that he can't see the backs of your thighs and compare them to the last supermodel he dated.

*

He's so young he won't remember Michael Jackson before he was white.

*

His pyjamas will have little *feet*.

*

He'll have trainer wheels on his car.

*

He chooses his cereal for the toy.

*

When you're in dominant position astride, your face will fall forward, giving you ten chins. The missionary means your breasts will fall to the side. (Solution? The dimmer switch. Greatest sex aid known to womankind.)

Older men

A beauty therapist recently offered me a massage with hot rocks. I declined. If I'm going to lie under a hot stone, I'd rather it was Mick.

Huon pines are not the oldest living thing on the planet. There are also the Beatles, the Rolling Stones and aged billionaires with a heart murmur.

*

I do suggest you stop this side of the grave (although with upper-class English men, how do you tell?).

*

Frequent auction houses. A *collector* of expensive antiques often turns out to *be* one. All a girl needs to do is pepper her conversation with 'Jacobean' this and 'Georgian' that and she'll soon be sending him 'baroque', while he furnishes her for life. So what are the pros and cons of becoming an antique cock collector?

Pros of dating older men

The best thing about marrying an older man with a coronary condition is that 'till death do us part' is less of a commitment.

*

Where there's a will, you can definitely be in it. There are three signs of senility – memory deterioration and . . . the other two have slipped his mind, right? 'Just sign on the dotted line, darling.'

*

What does it matter if the face has slipped, as long as the penis is in the right place?

*

Cons of dating older men

The man's not distinguished, he's extinguished. He'll be wheeled into bed sucking on an oxygen mask.

*

Because he has a walk-in wallet, occasionally women risk bedroom botulism by going out with a man who has passed his amuse-by date. But older men are often cut from the same tweedy mixture of snobbery and violence that supplied the warp and weft of British empire-builders.

*

Refrain from correcting his jargon and slang. Try not to laugh when he brags that he '*went high*' and got '*on* his face'. And remember, after he delivers an enlightened spiel on marijuana legalization, don't gush, 'God! I wish my dad was like you!' Or 'When you were young . . . gulp . . . ger.' Such slips send them scurrying off for double doses of Viagra and ginseng.

*

You'll have to put up with people making cracks along the lines of 'What's he got? The 70-year-old itch?' or 'He's so ancient. I mean, how did you meet? No, no. Let me guess. You bid on him at an auction?'

English upper-class men

In England, even the letters travel first and second class. Do the first-class letters get a little in-flight movie and a cocktail with a paper parasol on the way? Upper-class men prefer their dogs to their children. They keep their dogs at home and send their kids off to high-class kennels called Eton and Harrow.

The trouble with upper-class English blokes is that they don't speak English. They speak *euphemism*. It's a surrogate mother tongue. You need those little United Nations headphones to decipher what everybody is saying to you. For example, 'You Australians are so re*fresh*ing' decodes as 'Rack off, you loud-mouthed colonial nymphomaniac.' (I know, how *dare* he call you a loud mouth!)

*

They're Conan the Grammarians. He'll even correct your grammar when you're talking dirty in bed.

*

The voice of the upper-class male is so brittle it qualifies for osteoporosis pills. He has an accent sharp enough to draw blood if you're shaving your armpits with it.

*

English men pluck their highbrows. They are poetry-quoting brainiacs. Been there, Donne that. You'll have to swot up on the bleeding heart plots of operas – a case of vocal haemophilia, in which the leads invariably get stabbed and then can't stop singing.

*

He'll never do anything spontaneous without a warning . . . Well, he may be planning a little spontaneity – perhaps tomorrow. His condoms are practically pinstriped. And he's not good at personal grooming. Piles of dandruff form around his ankles.

*

If an upper-class man puts you in the 'blue room', it's because this will be the colour of your lips as you freeze to death. At least you won't have to go outside for a breath of fresh air. Their plan is that you'll have to have frottage, just to stave off frostbite.

*

Upper-class men don't marry for love. There's always a life-guard by their gene pool. Their bible is *Debrett's*, a book listing everybody who's anybody. It'll tell you all about their property and pedigree. (In Australia, breeding is something we do with sheep.)

*

You have to perform open-heart surgery before knowing what goes on inside an upper-class Englishman.

*

The trouble with such Englishmen is that they've all got corrugated bottoms from being beaten so much at boarding school. Put it this way: he'll make an impression on your mind . . . from the bottom up.

*

Even though he's constantly rushing off to brothels to be whipped with bits of wet lettuce, he'll have you arrested for wearing underwear above your station.

*

His approach to co-parenting is that it should be divvied up equally – between the boarding school and the nanny.

*

They have facial expressions by Taxidermy.

*

What he sees as compellingly eccentric, you may see as full on certifiable.

American Men

American Romeos don't romance any more, they 'relate'. Many belong to the Iron John movement, where they hug trees and get in touch with their 'fundamental masculinity' . . . Basically I've never known a man to take a hand *off* his fundamental masculinity for more than two minutes a day.

French men

A French man's love is like his central heating; it may keep you warm, but is nothing more than hot air. 'The poetry of your soul is in your eyes' is just French for 'You're ugly – but it's late so I'll shag you anyway.'

French charm is like mayonnaise: you definitely need something else to go with it.

Italian Men

Italian men are fluent in body language. They have the gift of the grab. He'll ask you up for 'coffee', but it's coffee in perverted commas.

Swedish Men

This is the sort of guy you could write home about – if your parents are into vodka chasers, flavoured French ticklers and doing it standing up backwards before a video camera.

Australian men

Romance Aussie style – an Aussie boyfriend once said to me, 'You're like toilet paper. It's the difference between scratching your arse and tearing it.' I looked at him, perplexed. 'Rough dunny paper's a dime a dozen. You are softest Sorbent.' Maybe that's why I fell for him. He was such a smooth-talking bastard.

*

Their humour is drier than an AA clinic. When I asked one boyfriend why he didn't show more emotion, he replied sardonically, 'Oh, you women. You want to be told how much we love you over and over again . . . At least two or three times a year. It's bloody exhausting.'

*

Most Aussie men are emotional bonsai. You have to whack on the fertilizer to get any feelings out of him.

*

He's uncomfortable with public displays of affection. The only thing he'll ever have his arm around in public is a beer glass. But there's a romantic streak in him. Buried. Like a seam of gold.

Despite the Croc Dundee image, most Aussies are urban dwellers. So don't fall in love with him because of his supposed outback ingenuity. The only way most Aussie blokes can make a fire by rubbing two sticks together is if one of them is a match.

Gay men

Coming out of the closet is a very courageous thing to do. It can take a man a long time to admit that he's strictly dickly. Hey, better latent than never. But do watch out for early warning signs. If your boyfriend can name non-standard colours and drinks soya decaf, he's probably a player of the pink piccolo. If the only stiff thing about him is his upper lip, then there's a good chance he's a vagina decliner. His motto will soon be 'Ditch the bitch and switch.'

*

It's the 21st century – behind every successful man is the Other Man.

*

If you discover that your bloke *is* coming out, don't try to push him back in again. Men never go off the gay and narrow.

Different expectations

Women want love and marriage and happy-ever-afters ... Most men want a 'meaningful' one-night stand – preferably with 7 bisexual hookers.

*

The way to impress a woman: tenderness, caressing, talking, devotion, trust, truth, togetherness.

How to impress a man:
1) Turn up naked.
2) Bring a naked double-jointed supermodel who owns a brewery and has an open-minded twin sister.
3) Wrestle in jelly.

Bad dates

Always best to go out on a few dates before committing to a weekend. Better you find out how boring he is *now* and not while on a walking tour of the Lake District.

*

Always remember, most men are like worms, only taller . . .

*

When dumped, this is your mantra: '*All Men Are Bastards and Evermore Shall Be So Unless They Are George Clooney Who Is Crumpet.*'

*

The only type of man you'll want to meet after a bad break-up is the one doused in petrol and with a stake driven through his heart.

*

If you meet a man who belittles his ex-wife – 'I *do* have an ex-wife, worst luck. Though you're welcome to refer to her by her real name: Spawn of Satan' – a few responses occur simultaneously:

1)   Why can't you see his electro-convulsive therapy scorch marks?

2) How the hell does he fit his cloven hooves into those trainers?

If things reach an all-time high in lows, you can always give up on men and just become lesbian. It *is* only a slip of the tongue.

Men to avoid

So many men and so many reasons not to date any of them. But unless you want to get carpal tunnel masturbation syndrome you have no option but to date. As there's a man shortage (most men seem to be married or gay, and the rest have a three-grunt vocabulary of 'na', 'dunno' and 'errgh'), we women would be satisfied with a man who has his own hair and no visible body piercings. But there are some men who have no redeeming features. (At least Nero could fiddle.) As I've had every oddball known to womankind (I could have a direct line to Jerry Springer), here is my guide to men to avoid. Hey, why give yourself an experience you'll have to pay a lot of money to a therapist to get over?

Avoid doctors

Most doctors are so terrified of disease they wear a condom while masturbating.

*

His idea of sexual inventiveness is not to wear his plastic anti-contamination gloves. He'll shower before taking a bath – in which he'll use separate washcloths on different parts of his body so as not to cross-contaminate from one orifice to the other. He'll gargle after oral sex. His body will be so sterile, a bacterium would die of loneliness. When making love, he'll stop at timed intervals to check his own pulse and respiration rate. Post-coitus, like a kindly children's GP he'll probably give you a jellybean for saying 'Aaaargh'.

*

The chief medical officer should issue a warning that marrying doctors can be seriously hazardous to your health.

Avoid jargon junkies . . .

Who use words like 'multi-tasking' and 'outsourcing' and other buzzwords like, well, 'buzzwords'. If he calls love an 'on-site merger', or an orgy an 'off-site team-building event', there's little doubt he'll call his wedding anniversary a 'performance review of core competencies', his children 'pilot projects' and the divorce you'll eventually demand 'emotional downsizing.'

Avoid famous men

A male celebrity thinks he's irresistible; success goes straight to his cock.

*

He keeps fit by doing step aerobics off his own ego.

*

He'll have love bites on his mirrors. He'll go through the tunnel of love holding his own hand. But women will still leap on him as though he's the last helicopter out of Saigon.

*

He'll be me-deep in conversation, singing his own praises for approximately eternity, before running through the history of his illustrious family since, oh, the Crusades.

*

If you marry such a man, instead of 'His and Her' hand towels it'll be more of a 'Me and Me' hand-towel situation. This is a man who suffers from *high* self-esteem. He'll do his crosswords in *ink*.

*

He's so vain he'll install a follow spotlight in his bedroom.

*

He's a braggart. If it's no sooner done than said, then you're sooner done with said bloke.

*

Man: 'So, what are you saying exactly? That I have a big ego?'
Woman: 'Oh, is *that* what's blocking out the sun?'

Avoid lawyers

Lawyers are workaholics – you'll soon be suffering from sub-poena envy.

*

The trouble with living with a human rights lawyer is that you can never get the high moral ground. When I was first married and asked my husband to change a nappy, he replied, 'But I've got 250 people on death row in Trinidad.' What could I say? But after 4,000 nappies, I retorted, 'Oh, let them die.' After the second baby, I was like – 'I'm going to go there and kill them myself. Human rights begin at home!'

*

Answer carefully in all arguments. He's a lawyer. He only needs another two signatures to put you away.

*

Wife: 'Um, actually, I don't want your opinion . . . and neither does anybody else in this cinema.'
Lawyer hubby: 'Don't be ludicrous. I'm a lawyer, everybody wants my opinion. I'm paid £250 an hour for it.'

*

He won't be able to talk dirty in bed, because if he talks he has to charge.

*

He'll soon have you plea-bargaining for foreplay. And out-lining all your sexual requirements in a counsel's notebook in which he'll write up a lengthy opinion.

*

If a lawyer's ego was hit by lightning, the lightning would be hospitalized.

*

Lawyers have been at Oxford for so long they have ivy grow-ing up the backs of their legs. And what they graduated in is Advanced Smugness. They have a Condescension Chromosome.

*

Lawyers tend to drown in their own brainwaves.

*

When you finally divorce, it won't so much be the end of a marriage as Case Closed.

Avoid family avoiders

If you love your family, best to avoid a man who thinks fami-lies are like Brussels sprouts – a dreary duty to be endured at Christmas. You think blood is thicker than water, but he thinks – hey, so is eggnog.

Avoid married men

There is no etiquette guide entitled *What to Do When Your Fiancé Is Still Married*. Of course, you never know he's married until you find the teething ring in his pocket, but by then you think love is in the air . . . Until it turns out to be the exhaust fumes of his sports car as he zooms back to his wife.

*

Man: 'Let's make love . . . And yes, of course we'll get married.'
Woman: 'Really? But I think your family will totally object. As in – *your bloody wife and children!*'

*

There always turns out to be a draught in his 'open' marriage.

*

You'll both have sex, but you're the only one who'll get screwed.

*

To a married man, sex means no more than exercise. Naked yoga. A jog he didn't have to go outside for. It's no more intimate than, say, a Pilates class for two. You're just a little something to break the monogamy.

When it comes to learning life's lessons, don't be a straight D student. Repeat after me. He's never going to leave his wife.

Avoid hedge fund managers

To err is human, but to really fuck things up requires a financial adviser. Going broke saving money is certainly an interesting approach.

*

Past a certain age, if you go out with a bloke and he has Van Gogh's 'Sunflowers' on the wall, it had better be because he paid 30 bloody million bucks for it! But rich men are often chronically stingy. He'll make you go Dutch at McDonald's.

Avoid vulgarians

When a man likes movies with 'Pork', 'Death' or 'II' in the title it's a sure sign that his underpants size is bigger than his IQ. (And we're *not* talking well endowed.) If his opening conversational gambit is to crush a beer can on his forehead, it's likely he's the type to see alcohol as a major food group. Dating a man like this is as good an idea as, say, playing leapfrog with a rhinoceros.

Avoid men who like domestic goddesses

Any woman who says she gets high on housework has obviously inhaled too much cleaning fluid. (Definition of a 'hostage'? A woman who has to cook for bloody visitors.) A real woman just dials her finger to the bone ordering takeaways or finds a toyboy who can cook. When you wish upon a Michelin star, dreams really can come true . . .

Avoid men who go out with models

Most models put the 'cat' into 'catwalk'. Modelling could be learned by an advanced rodent. She's little more than a sabretoothed tapeworm. Of course, the reason models are so mean is because they're starving hungry. If they swallow a breadcrumb they think they look pregnant. They order one crouton for lunch – then share it. For a real treat, the woman might lick a sultana. Where do they keep their internal organs? In their handbags? They're so thin, their pyjamas have, like, *one* stripe. I once saw a model eating solids. 'I'm eating to compensate,' she mumbled between chews.

What for? *Hunger?*

*

A model will practically close a restaurant for serving whole milk in her skinny latte. 'Are you trying to *kill* me? The cholesterol. OHMYGOD.' A spritzer for her is half Perrier and half Volvic. The hypocrisy of only drinking flat mineral water to keep her inner self pure – while poisoning her system with Botox – is totally lost on her.

*

What does it say about a man who would go out with a woman like this? That he's had a DIY lobotomy, that's what.

Avoid male models . . .

Who wear sunglasses at night, have sex on vinyl sheets and boast of their individuality, while looking identical. Male models only believe in one minority group – millionairesses.

Avoid girlfriend avoiders

Beware men who think that the only women who need girl-friends are lesbians. Girlfriends should have a pact to 'never to let a penis come between us'. Men may come (the nights they don't have brewer's droop) and go but it's your female mates who last for ever.

Avoid men with pick-up lines

(No matter how cute his buns.) 'Hi babe. How 'bout a sixty-eighter? Go down on me and I'll owe you one,' etc. is a definite indication that he normally goes out with the sort of female you inflate by blowing into her toe.

Avoid men with fancy cars

Four-wheeled land cruisers scream 'pretentious wanker'. Alfas say '*rich* pretentious wanker'. Ferraris, Maseratis and Lamborghinis? Well, they're obviously tax-dodgem cars. But nothing speaks quite so loudly as a red Porsche. And what it's saying is – meno-Porsche. His number plate should read 'Midlife Crisis'.

*

Never get into a car whose bumper sticker reads 'God is my Pilot'. The dice dangling from his rear-view mirror will be loaded.

Avoid double-adaptors

Avoid the type who only tells you halfway through your amorous encounter about his operation. Sorry, *her* operation. At a gender realignment clinic. Basically, he's shooting eggs into you. It pays to be more discriminating. Before going out with a man, always ask yourself one very important question: 'Does he have his own penis?'

Avoid unemotional men

You're not having a 'relationship'. Just 365 one-night stands with the same person.

*

These men confine affection to times of erection.

*

He probably has a pet name for his penis. (A male preserve. I've never been informally introduced to a vagina.)

Avoid fat men

Trying to locate the love muscle of an overweight man in the dark is a little like attempting to land on an aircraft carrier in a hurricane without radar.

Avoid lazy men

If he's currently looking for a job which has office hours from one to two with an hour off for lunch, your HMS relation-ship has a touch of the *Titanics*.

Avoid psychiatrists

Psychology is nothing more than a guess with a degree. There has to be something amiss in an industry where the customer is always wrong. Surely we can think of more fun things to do on a sofa?

Avoid criminals

He'll pick pockets at your family reunions, believing that every crowd has a silver lining. He'll go through your purse, believing that the change will do him good. If you want an off-beat record collection, go for classical, not criminal. Any children you have will follow in their father's fingerprints.

Avoid pessimists

Such men have mastered the art of negative thinking. He has post-natal depression – his own. His blood type is B minus. He may even manufacture arguments because he likes nothing more than optimum brooding conditions. He thinks optimism is an eye disease. Eeyore-ish men see the bad side of everything. If he had his way, he'd be skywriting 'There is no such thing as Santa!' over Euro Disney.

Avoid the overly charming

The guy may be more disarming than a team of UN weapons inspectors, but it's often nothing more than the art of genital persuasion. He's friendly in the way an intestinal parasite is friendly. He's a top-order predator – meaning he'll say 'thank you' before spiking your drink with Rohypnol.

Avoid royals

They're just the winners in the Lucky Sperm competition.

Avoid surfies

As surfie chicks, we folded their towels, bought their Chicko Rolls, minded their milkshakes, turtle-backed ('Once you're on your back, you're fucked,' the boys said) and got tan tattoos. The boys made us cut their names out of a sheet of paper, Sellotape it on to our tummies then sunbathe to get a tan tattoo in the shape of his name. If I ever get cancer I'll have a melanoma called Bruce. I'll have to undergo a Bruce-ectomy.

*

A surfie's party trick is to get drunk and set his pubic hairs alight.

*

A surfie is a walking, talking life-support system to a wetsuit.

Avoid name-droppers

He should get his jaw rewired to allow even bigger names out. He'll drop you too as soon as a bigger name comes along.

Avoid bikers

The bubonic plague would take antibiotics before setting foot in this bloke's system. Every time he peels off a sock, the entire room will take on the fungal humidity of a fridge you accidentally turned off while away on holiday. Men like this could introduce a whole range of hideous bacterial organisms into your reproductive system.

*

He won't have been to the dentist for twenty years. When tongue kissing, he'll get you to check his upper left molar. He won't just have plaque on his teeth, but *plankton*.

Avoid chauvinists . . .

Who refer to women as cows or silly moos. There's a very good reason why men like this can't get mad cow disease . . . because they're pigs. What's the difference between men and pigs? Pigs don't get drunk and act like men. But just remember, it's pointless telling chauvinist jokes if you still marry one.

Avoid men who call themselves feminists

Men only called themselves feminists in the hope of getting a more intelligent bonk. If a bloke calls himself a 'new man', it's just a *phrase* he's passing through.

*

He's probably the sort of male feminist who thinks the 'glass ceiling' is a club for coprophiliacs. Explain to him that not only does the glass ceiling exist but women are paid four bucks an hour less than men to dust it while we're up there.

*

The trouble with born-again new men is that they're an even bigger pain in the bum the second time round.

Avoid inebriates

The only thing he can really grasp in an argument is a beer can.

Avoid overly hairy men who whine when you don't wax

Naked, he looks like a fur ball that something has vomited up. When he was born, he got carpet burn from his mother's thighs. He doesn't have mere stubble, but more your basic Harris tweed. Yet he wants *you* as hairless as a lab rat? Wax lyrical instead about how it's time you skulked back to your lair.

Avoid men who are users

He's so reliable – always there when he needs you.

Avoid anal retentives

These men hug their *shoetrees*. They're spontaneity-impaired. His culinary highlight involves massaging his bowel with bran flakes. A girl wants a man who doesn't worry during oral sex whether or not his decay-preventative dental hygiene programme is effective enough.

Men like this are more controlling than Elizabeth Taylor's pantyhose.

Avoid wine bores

Men who put the bore into Bordeaux should come stamped with a warning – 'May Cause Drowsiness'.

*

His photographic palate will be able to distinguish the area, the year, the grape, the soil . . . *probably the picker's name*, for Christ's sake . . . and it'll be about as interesting as Bulgarian daytime television.

Avoid any member of the Mile High Club . . .

When flying solo. If your plane crashed in the Himalayas and you had plenty of rations and a rescue helicopter had been spotted, you'd *still* eat him, just because he's so damn annoying.

Avoid exercise junkies

My only rules about sport are: nothing involving water, balls, my feet leaving the earth or sweat. My preferred activity is reading, in which there is not much potential for death. The hardest thing about push-ups is trying not to spill your wine . . . My main anxiety in life is that the evil prick who thought up aerobics classes might be thinking up something else right now, the sadistic bastard. But some women invariably fall for the 'Excuse me while I do the six-hundred-metre butterfly, climb two Alps and rappel back down for some dressage and parachute formation before lunch' types. If you *do* fall for a sports junkie, the most important sports to avoid are:

*

Scuba Diving   If God had meant us to swim in the ocean, he would have given us shark-proof metal cages. I mean, there must be a reason fish never look truly relaxed – *because something much, much bigger is always trying to devour them.*

*

Waterskiing   The art of knocking down a jetty with your face, and hence the mainstay of neurosurgeons worldwide.

*

Swimming   The trouble with swimming is that one gets so wet. If the sea were a woman's natural habitat there'd be waterproof shoeshops.

*

Walking   Don't expect to lose weight unless you walk through at least three time zones daily. Tell him if you have to lose something you'd rather it were your inhibitions, then simply take a walk on the wild side.

*

Jogging   The only thing I run up are bills. I *have* been known to run – but only when my flat was on fire. I once entered the London Marathon. People thought I'd won . . . until they realized that I was just finishing last year's race. You're so exhausted that you feel sure that at one point you passed Greenland.

*

If God had meant us to run on roads, he'd have given us four-wheeled feet.

*

Yoga If a man tells you to get in touch with your body, explain that your body is not all that communicative. 'If I *do* hear from it, I'll let you know, OK?' Or find a really crowded aerobics class and wedge yourself between two female athletes, allowing them to do all the bounding and jumping. They'll simply carry you along. Or take up yoga. I do like an exercise regime which allows you to lie down and go to sleep.

Avoid men who push you into cosmetic surgery

Los Angeles is a wrinkle-free zone. There is no law of gravity. Skin sags *upwards*. Basically, they just drag everything up. Your ankles become your knees. Your knees your navel. Your clitoris becomes your chin. That's how you spot a recipient of cosmetic surgery. You look for a woman who is rubbing that particular part of her anatomy a little too vigorously.

*

Dump any man who wants you to have younger skin. What beauticians call dermabrasion most of us know by its original term: medieval torture. Why pay thousands to have your face resemble a burnt pizza? And why destroy the years of goodlookingness you have left, by worrying about staying good-looking?

*

Do you really want to become one of those women who is approaching 40, but from the wrong direction? There'll be bits of your body that you've had operated on that don't go with the bits which *haven't* been. Your arms will be over four decades old and your lips, two weeks. You'll be sitting on one brand-new butt cheek while the other half of your arse is forty-two.

*

My mother told me never to pick my nose – especially from a catalogue.

*

The only plastic surgery a woman should experience is cutting up the credit card she was going to use to pay for that shopping and tucking.

*

Cowboy cosmetic surgeons are not real doctors. Most couldn't put a dressing on a salad. The reason doctors wear those little green masks is that, if anything goes wrong, they won't be recognized.

*

At least we know why they call what they do a *practice*. I mean, how did cosmetic surgeons become doctors? By correspondence course? Who did they train under – Dr Seuss?

*

Cosmetic surgeons don't perform unnecessary surgery . . . they only operate if they need the money.

*

So forget facelifts. Men should learn to read between your lines.

*

Facelifts are a stitch in time. Now that really would have confused Einstein.

*

And just remember, skin has only one function. It's to stop your insides from slopping out everywhere.

*

The bottom line is, why would you want a man who only wants you because you're silicone from tit to toe?

Avoid men who criticize your weight

Avoid a man who tells you to lose a bit round the thighs. It hasn't stopped him from parting them, now has it?

*

If he says you're so fat that whales come to watch *you*; that your butt has its own zip code; that Christo uses your raincoat to wrap islands in, etc. – just tell him that it took a lot of self-control and determination but you've managed to give up dieting. If he can find a diet that doesn't actually involve eating less you'll talk, OK? (My alternative dieting tip – place spaghetti strands vertically on your plate, for a more slimming effect.) Or just cook him and eat him.

*

Trying to be thin for a man means sucking your stomach in so violently your neck will get thicker.

*

Of course, you could always try bulimia – a case of having your cake and throwing it up too. Yes, bulimia gives you a figure to die for – literally.

*

Do you know how models get themselves to vomit up their food? They just listen to themselves *talk*.

*

If Mother Nature had wanted our skeletons to be visible, I have a strong suspicion that she would have put them on the outside of our bodies.

*

End world hunger – eat a model.

*

Have too much lipo and your vagina could finish up askew – then you really will be a 'little bit on the side'.

*

Fridge-o-suction is a much more useful technique . . . Just suck the food right out of the refrigerator at source.

Avoid footballers

OK, he has a great body. You could bivouac in the shade of this man's penis. But footballers are big for their brains like dinosaurs. Footballers were given their brain for nothing. Just a spinal column would have done.

*

Footballers treat you just like a football – they make a pass, play footsie – then drop you as soon as they've scored.

Avoid rock stars

Lock up your daughters, dogs and all household plants. The rock star is back in town.

*

The band may be way ahead of its time . . . or perhaps just late.

*

To date a rock star, you must serve the probationary two-year bulimia period.

*

A rock star's girlfriend is the reverse of an iceberg: 90 per cent of her is visible. Most of it between clit and clavicle.

*

You'll have to wear so much jungle print clothing that you'll need to take malaria tablets.

*

Your sequinned boob tube and lycra hot pants is a look that doesn't quite come off . . . but definitely gives the impression that it will later. Probably for the *whole band*.

*

How many rock stars does it take to screw in a light bulb? One: rock stars will screw anything.

*

To a rock star, a woman is nothing more than a mattress with breasts – something he can lie down on while having a shag.

*

The man's underpants could be inducted into the Hall of Infamy. He beds so many girls he needs a *placement* on his *pillows*.

*

There'll be hordes of young women in awed orbit around the band. It will look like a training class for those innocuous, smiling female quiz-show sidekicks – 'Ladies and gentlemen, a *car*.' Most of these women look as though they just crawled out from under a rolling stone . . . probably Keith.

*

They go out with the kind of woman who would sell the tabloid press slides of her cervical smear test if the price was right.

*

Even though he has the most prodigious organ outside Westminster Abbey, a rock star's brain is just that thing he thinks he thinks with.

*

The reason rock and roll bands tour is because no one knows what a nonentity they are back home, and no one back home knows what a nonentity they are on tour.

*

A rock star is a member of the Illiterati. His catch cry: how gauche it with you?

Avoid the strong, silent type

When looking for a representative of the ring-buying sex, avoid the strong, silent type. At first you think men like this are perfect as they're so self-contained. Until you discover that he has the emotions of a Vulcan. The guy probably goes home at night and peels his face off.

* * * * *

That's the basic list of bottom-feeders. Now you must vow to never lower your standards again – well, not unless you are so moist from sexual arousal that the chair is getting up when *you* do.

What women really want

What are women looking for? Oh, nothing special. As long as he has pectorals, a Ph.D., a nice bum, a non-sexist attitude, a top tan, can cook soufflés, arm-wrestle crocodiles, wants a loving relationship and can provide bone-marrow-melting sex because he's hooked up intravenously to a copy of the Kama Sutra . . . Now, is that too much to ask of a billionaire?

*

Women want a Knight in Shining Armani who is good at wordplay. In other words, a man who can shop and mop and find your G-spot – while constantly thrusting away with his rapier.

*

Women want to date a historian – as he'll never think you're too old.

*

A woman wants a man who can meet her needs – in other words, a heterosexual haute-couture designer with a ten-inch tongue who can breathe through his ears.

CHAPTER 2

Sex

Sex

Men think about sex all day. For all his declarations of love, he's little more than a heat-seeking penis which does not report to Mission Control.

*

Most men like to have sex when they're sad. They like to have sex when they're lonely. They like to have sex when they're happy. They like to have sex when it's raining. They like to have sex when it's steamy and hot. They like to have sex in the morning. They like to have sex in the evenings. They like to have sex in trains, planes and automobiles. They like to have tantric sex for hours and hours. They like to have quick-fix sex standing up backwards over the kitchen table. Otherwise, they don't have sex unless they're really, really horny.

*

For many men it's any orifice in a storm.

*

Men will put their dicks where women wouldn't put an umbrella.

*

Men will shag anything. Including body-temperature pies or tethered, reasonably domesticated livestock.

*

As long as it's warm and still breathing, many men will shag it – then count the legs afterwards.

*

Men always think women are hot for them. You could be stabbing a man repeatedly with a carving knife in the cardio-artery-vascular thingy and he'd still be thinking, 'Oh, wow, she really fancies me!'

*

Men either come too quickly, or take too long. Premature ejaculators or Oh-my-God-the-ceiling-needs-painting ejaculators.

*

Male mystique – that indefinable something about a hot-to-trot young spunk rat with a huge appendage.

The penis

It's not women who suffer from penis envy, but men. It's men who agonize about size. Is mine big? Is it the biggest?

*

And while a well-endowed man is a joy to behold (a sequoia tree takes two hundred years to attain the same girth it takes men to achieve in an instant at the merest glimpse of a fishnet stocking), we women don't just sit around discussing the length of a man's manhood . . . We also discuss the *width*, which, after childbirth, is much, much more important.

*

Penises, like snowflakes, are each of them different. And women like them all. We like them in all shapes and sizes. The lean, slinky, kinky ones. The thick, succulent types. The low-slung, gunslinger sort. The stubby button mushrooms. The round-heads. The hooded eyes. The meat and two veg, packed-lunch variety. We like them long and strong and ready for action. We like them all coy on a cold winter's morning. All this male agony over size, when it's *attitude* women are interested in. Women like a penis which says, 'G'day! God, am I glad to see *you*!'

*

But it's best to reassure him. Just choose from the following:
1) That's not a penis. That's a vaulting pole!
2) Your penis is so big it's in a separate time zone to your body.
3) Your appendage looks as though it should be on a launch pad at Cape Canaveral awaiting blast-off . . .

*

Also reassure him that a penis can be too big. A beef bayonet which could double as a draught excluder does not look good in a girl.

*

But if a man brags about his appendage, simply deflate him with these few simple words. 'Sorry, I'm not into "small talk".'

Flirting

Men are like fish. Chuck 'em the right bait and you've got 'em by the gills.

*

But just because a woman is flirting doesn't mean she wants to sleep with a man. I mean, does a dog actually plan to catch the car it's chasing? No, it's just habit. But flirt with a man and he'll think you want him. Most men think inanimate objects want them.

*

So don't give out wrong signals. There is only one reason a man ever gives a woman a key to his room – and it isn't to hem a curtain.

*

Upper-class foreplay: 'I'll let you play with my hyphen if I can play with yours.'

*

When a man asks you to say, 'Tell me I'm the only one, babe,' it's a pretty good indication that his idea of fidelity is only having one woman in bed at a time.

*

Beware flirting with rich men. He knows that money talks, and what he wants it to say is 'Hi, I'm from Planet Shag.'

Types of sex

There are three types of sex:
1) Brand new, kitchen table sex.
2) Bedroom sex.
3) Hallway sex, when you pass each other in the hallway and say 'Fuck you.'

Light and shade

Some men insist on turning out the light. As you go through the motions in the dark, you'll gradually realize that he's actually having sex with Britney Spears . . . and she's getting many more orgasms than you are.

One-night stands

One night stand: hips that pass in the night.

*

Men can make love to a perfect stranger. Except he won't want you to be perfect. He'll want you to be really dirty and bad.

*

Women think, why go to bed with a stranger? He won't know who or what is on the end of his penis. You could be a carton of curdled custard.

*

I don't like casual sex. I like it as formal as possible. Blood tests, CVs, the works.

*

The downside to a one-night stand is that you'll awake to find your arm wedged under his hairy torso. You're caught like a dingo in a trap. He's what's known in Australian female folklore as a 'dingo man' – the sort of guy who makes you feel you'd rather gnaw your arm off than have to wake him up and talk to him.

*

The truth is, sexual liberation can be very oppressive. Vaginal, clitoral, multiple . . . It's a genital dictatorship. We've all become so anxious about how we're being laid, we've somehow mislaid the essential ingredients of romance, adoration, devotion.

Kinks

Beware the man who thinks that sex is nobody's business, except for the horse, dog, wife and two hookers involved.

*

If a man gets into bed with a jar of Vaseline it's not because he's planning to swim the English Channel.

*

Making love in the carwash during the wax/dry cycle is the true definition of autoeroticism.

*

Trying new things sexually creates such terrible eye wrinkles caused by puckering up into a squint and shouting, 'You want me to do WHAT?' And, I'm sorry, but surely handcuffs are only acceptable if you're an undercover cop with Scotland Yard. The very thought of group sex makes me suffer from a performance anxiety I haven't felt since those hedonistic hours of enforced folk dancing in primary school. (The only good thing about an orgy is that it does away with the anxiety about what to wear.) And don't you think inflating plastic sexual-pleasure enhancers must cause the most awful migraines? I also have little doubt that fishnet friction can inflict a nasty wound on your groin area. Nor do I want the persistent pneumonia, which comes from constantly slipping into something less comfortable. A shaved pudendum may sound erotic, but when it's growing back it looks like a shag pile that's been terrorized.

*

Besides, what woman wants third-degree carpet burns on bits of her anatomy that can't be explained away as a housework-related incident? Or a rope burn which comes under the category of the Most Humiliating Chafe Mark in the History of the Universe?

Bondage

I'd always presumed bondage was just an inventive way of keeping your partner from going home too early.

*

The only thing I've ever whipped is cream.

*

When his foreplay includes tethering you to the chair with an Old Etonian tie, point out that you've read *Who's Who* and you know he went to Leek Boys High. Then leave. You really don't want to get pregnant to a man like this. Pretentious snobberies are hereditary.

*

Hey, if suspenders are so great, guys would be wearing them. Which brings me to . . .

Cross-dressing

When my girlfriend discovered her husband in her best Dolce

& Gabbana skirt, she was gutted, furious and profoundly mortified. 'How could he *do* that? He was wearing stockings with sandals!'

Toys

If a man's sex toy collection includes a row of gigantic clenched fists attached to plastic forearms, it's *not* for political rallies.

*

The Ben Wa brochure he gave you promises orgasmic bliss. But what it doesn't say is that inserting these chrome bowling balls will be like childbirth, only backwards. And with no epidural. And once you put them in, will you ever get them out again? If not, you're in for the most embarrassing airport security search ever.

*

You may try to develop some kinks, like wearing his underwear or going commando. But, as a mother of two with no pelvic floor, one must be cautious about not wearing any knickers. What if your Ben Wa ball falls out during a staff meeting? The only way out is to pretend to be a player of miniature bowling.

Aussie men

The Australian definition of foreplay is shearing. Which gives new meaning to heavy petting.

Indian men

The Kama Sutra is a short work of fiction, judging by the Indian men I know. Most men think the Kama Sutra is some kind of Indian takeaway.

English men

An English man may wear triple-breasted tweed condoms, but he'll also be a member of a mutual aberration society. He can probably only achieve an erection when touched on the genitals by a rubberized gardening glove.

*

That's the trouble with English men – they just can't drive past a perversion without pulling over.

*

The 'cream of English society' just means rich, thick and prone to whipping. But the trouble with the cream of society is that it often curdles.

*

The English male has an obsession with sado-masochism. I suppose it's because the winters are long and playing charades and bridge do get boring after a while. But I'm sure I speak for all women when I say that we don't like to be beaten – not even at Monopoly!

Toyboys

Ask any married woman the difference between a husband

and a toyboy and she'll tell you the same thing. About three hours.

*

It'll be as if you've suddenly found yourself in one of those subtitled European movies. The man will make love to you as though you're an endangered species. You'll be having so many flights of fancy, you'll need to file flight plans. 'All aboard. Your flight of fancy is approaching takeoff. Your exits are . . .' – but hey, who would want to leave? As you run your hands over his satiny, bronzed skin and kiss his dreamy, creamy eyelids, remind yourself that growing old is compulsory. Growing up is optional.

*

But beware. During a romantic encounter, if you casually remark that he's skilled enough to do it professionally, he may reply that he *is* and that the payment will be fifty quid. It's then you notice the VFM tattooed on his penis: 'Value For Money'.

Married sex

The trouble with married sex is not women faking orgasm but men faking foreplay.

*

If a husband does attempt a little half-hearted foreplay, he invariably prods away at your clit as though it's an elevator button and he's running late for a meeting. It is then that a woman might cut to the carnal chase and sigh, exasperatedly, 'Oh, just take the stairs.'

*

Without doubt, husbands and wives approach sex differently. What men call a 'quickie', most women would dismiss as premature ejaculation. Some men are so premature their wives are not even in the room. So who was he fantasizing about? How *could* he let Sarah Palin have sex in your bedroom!

*

Your husband thinks he's a real animal in bed. He is. *A hamster*.

*

For most married couples, being creative in bed means knitting while watching *Newsnight*.

*

Married sex – *pre*-coital depression.

*

Husbands are to wives what condoms are to sex. They kill all sensation.

*

The only rash thing about a husband is his eczema. You appear wearing your lingerie with latex trapdoors dripping honey into your navel and sugar-coating both nipples – and he keeps reading his *Telegraph*. 'Sorry, what were you saying?' he'll mutter. 'Something about me not noticing you any more?'

*

Although I don't call it 'being noticed' when he pounces on you with the words 'We've just got time to do it, I've got the bath running.' Or arrives with two cups of coffee, for *afterwards*.

*

All this fuss about sex before marriage. What about sex after marriage? Once, having loads of sex made a woman feel guilty and cheap. After marriage, NOT having loads of sex makes a woman feel guilty and cheap.

*

A year or two of marriage and all he'll give you between the sheets is an anticlimax.

*

The sexual titillation between spouses sometimes becomes so intense that couples are tempted to flick on the telly to watch the darts final.

*

Wives are often so bored in bed they take to calculating exactly how many shoes they own. (82 pairs.) Oh, the things you can fathom when time is on your side!

*

Even though women make up 50 per cent of the workforce we still do 99 per cent of all housework and childcare. By the time an exhausted mum finally slumps into bed, the one thing she's fantasizing about is sleep. And oh, how her heart sinks when she's sliding into slumber and suddenly feels *the Hand*.

*

Men make horror movies about the Blob or the Alien or The Thing. What terrorizes men is Wolfman, the Zombie, Dracula, Frankenstein. What terrorizes *women*, well, weary mothers at least, is *the Hand*.

*

It would appear that your husband, the man who hasn't spoken to you all night or helped with the dishes, thinks that you're in the mood for love. What you're in the mood for is running him through with a carving knife.

*

A tired wife will do everything to discourage her husband, bar stretching razor wire around her bed and setting bait traps. A wife wearing saggy, baggy flannelette pyjamas and airline socks to bed is the sexual equivalent of World War Two soldiers laying minefields across the entrance to their tunnels.

*

The reply most wives would give to a husband who said that he wanted to make love to her so badly would be 'Um, darling, I think you succeeded.'

*

There comes a time in every marriage when a slow-drip sexual ennui sets in and lovemaking becomes more dutiful than enthusiastic. It's been so long since many married women have had sex, they'd probably get motion sickness and have to tell their husbands to pull the bed over to the kerb.

*

So, what happened to those days when you took headboard divots out of walls, broke beds and ran up chiropractic bills? In the first few years of marriage, couples are at it like rabbits. So what's with the marital myxomatosis?

*

A woman's sex life definitely deteriorates with the onset of motherhood. Despite the beanbags and the water births and the plinky, plonky harp music, giving birth still boils down to a doctor putting a knee on your chest, spreading your legs and diving in with a pair of barbecue tongs. While men want the tumbling in the hay to recommence six weeks after childbirth, mothers want to tie up the sheaves and put them in the barn.

*

Giving birth is traumatic enough, but no sooner have the lactation leakage circles dried on your shirtfront than your husband wants nookie. Needless to say, the woman with the recently stitched perineum does not.

*

A new mum is so tired she has to hire someone to have her orgasms for her.

*

For most new mums a new position in bed means sleeping on her other side.

*

New mums contemplate a subtle little hint to let him know she's not in the mood – like smashing a ceramic ashtray over his head.

*

Even if you do want to make love, children are a contraceptive. Every time you go to make love, the toddler toddles in. Try Vaseline. On the doorknobs. Sounds painful but they can't get in!

*

Wives aren't faking orgasms, they're *flunking* them. On those official Name/Address/Age forms, where it says Sex most wives should write 'NOT IF I CAN POSSIBLY HELP IT.'

*

With the onset of parenthood, women develop innovative ways of getting out of sex:

1) Taking a child into the marital bed because of a nightmare. (The playing of scary videos before bed greatly helps in this department.)

2) Asking your husband what position he'd like to do it in . . . then laughing hysterically when he answers.

3) Simply explaining that you can only really enjoy sex if you bring along your best friend… before revealing that your best friend is a gay manicurist called Merlyn.

4) Finishing all your sentences with 'in accordance with the prophecy'. (Although that could also lead to divorce. Or the sudden appearance of a few more wives.)

5) If you're really desperate for a good night's sleep, just when hubby's snuggling up, mention casually that the tax department rang wanting to audit his accounts. Not only will he lose the inclination for sex, he'll also lose the desire for sleep, which means you won't have to put up with his snoring either!

*

The good thing about having a baby: you don't have to make love for months afterwards. To most wives 'sexual freedom' means the freedom not to have sex. 'Not tonight, darling, I'm Having It All in the morning.'

*

It would seem that a new mum's favourite position is the 'doggy position' – where he begs . . . and she just rolls over and plays dead.

*

I used to think 'weaker sex' referred to the male of the species, but 'weaker sex' actually means the kind of sex you have after childbirth.

*

Ask a married couple whether they like the lights on or off and most would sensibly answer, 'On,' so they can read. As for talking dirty? Well, we mothers talk dirty all the time, as we order our children to wash their hands before dinner and point out that their rooms are a pigsty.

*

Sex therapists would no doubt diagnose an arousal disorder. What I diagnose is a demanding work schedule, two messy kids and a lazy husband. Men should understand that there are only a few basic ways to please a woman – stacking the dishwasher and not snoring.

*

A woman's biggest fantasy in the bedroom involves discovering that her husband has picked his underpants up off the floor.

*

Women go off sex due to exhaustion. If men did more housework, wives would have energy for other things. Oh, the orgasmic joy of being made love to by a man who has just hoovered your entire house!

*

All women dream of being taken. Well, we're being 'taken' all right, but not quite in the muscular-thighed, half-naked Adonis way we've wet-dreamed of. No, we're just being taken for granted, taken for a ride and, after divorce, to the cleaners.

*

Just help with the housework, boys, and your wife will be stretching as contentedly as a cat, eager to show you her appreciation. And it will be oh, OH, OHHHH WHAT A FEELING!

*

Sex in marriage . . . well, it's like when it slips your mind that you've put your windscreen wipers on intermittent. You've forgotten about it and then – WHOOSH!

*

Meanwhile, if your husband suggests that you could initiate sex now and again and perhaps even swap positions occasionally, simply reply, 'Yes, let's swap positions . . . *You* stand by the sink washing up and *I'll* lie on the couch drinking wine and watching the telly.'

Good sex — what women want

The female orgasm is more of a mystery than the career success of George W. Bush. But, by God, you have the right to have an Academy Award-winning one before *he* does.

*

A woman wants a man who kisses her so long and so lusciously that when he finally pulls away, she has to check she still has her pants on. We don't just want a kiss. We want mouth-to-mouth resuscitation . . . We want kisses that require a lifeguard. We want a man who will drag us into his mouth, descale our teeth, tickle our tonsils and become intimately acquainted with both sets of molars before detaching himself from us with the sound of a squid being prised off glass. This could lead to full stomach-to-stomach resuscitation.

*

We want a man who says the words every woman fantasizes about one day hearing (along with 'Scientists have discovered that celery is fattening'): 'Pleasing you is what gives me pleasure.'

*

Women want a man who can find our G-spot without a map, a compass and a list of edible berries.

*

If men were better in bed, women would want to spend more time there. Teach your man to find libidinous places where you didn't even know you *had* places. Encourage him to be a carnal cartographer, mapping out your erogenous zones – and then double-parking in all of them.

*

A woman wants nuzzling that makes her nipples so erect she can pick up the BBC World Service.

*

A woman wants an orgasm so strong that when she cries out she won't be sure whether it's an orgasm or demonic possession. Should you have a post-coital cigarette or call an exorcist?

*

What women want is a man so sexy he could open a deposit account at a sperm bank.

*

Women want to be made so high from orgasmic bliss that they can wave to the International Space Station.

*

But do you know what a woman really wants in bed? Breakfast.

What men want

Men want a woman with a trick pelvis. Men want a pelvis that can pull a rabbit out of a hat.

What women don't want

Men who think 'mutual orgasm' is an insurance company.

*

Premature ejaculation. If your man comes too early, tell him to delay orgasm by thinking of something awful. If he thinks about accidentally bumping into his mother-in-law at a nudist beach, he could delay orgasm by at least three months.

*

Women like to be hugged occasionally when we're not horizontal. Otherwise we suffer from an affection deficiency.

*

To be coerced into sex. Having sex when your heart isn't in it feels as though a party is being thrown in your body to which you haven't been invited.

*

Having sex when you're not in the mood is like dancing with no music.

Outdoor sex

Frostbite of the breasts, leeches on the labia and neck cramp from trying to keep one eye peeled for wandering psychopaths do *not* get a girl as aroused as her partner might think.

Orgies

There are quite a few overrated items and events in this world. Water beds, weddings, oysters, tattoos and group gropes. I mean, how can you have a good time when you're desperately jealous that everyone else is having a better time than you? All feelings of mutual sharing and caring evaporate when you find yourself sleeping in the wet patch . . . then realize that it's not your own.

*

Is there anything worse than listening to other people having sex? To the wet, gasping sounds of harpooned whales surfacing simultaneously? When in a group grope, take along a novel for the boring bits. Or a crossword. Maybe a manicure set? Who can relax when someone might leave wearing your designer Moschino? Worst thing is having to write the thank-you letters. 'Thank you for coming.' Or *not*.

Bad sex

When your orgasms haven't been clitoral or vaginal. But futile.

*

When his only attempt to find your G-spot leads to a totally humiliating trip to the Accident and Emergency department.

Faking it

There's little point in encouraging a male partner in practices which are not going to get you anywhere. By anywhere I mean the usually desired female destination of over the moon, off the edge of the planet or into another orbit entirely. But all women fake it a little *tiny* bit. Not in a grand, theatrical *When Harry Met Sally* kind of way. But, face it, when women wank, do they call out, 'Oh God! Don't stop! Oh! Oh! *OH!* Give it to me, big boy!' It's all theatrics, to some degree. But . . .

*

If you're bored and waiting for the ordeal to be over, *never* go limp, ooh and ah and writhe for a bit, then make a low moan and lie still because, impressed by his own sexual virtuosity, he's just as likely to say, 'You're going to have another seven of those!' and set to work again immediately.

*

Women just don't have Academy Award-winning orgasms with no foreplay.

*

Most men are good with their hands. They can fashion a temporary cistern ball float with a squeezy bottle and a coat hanger in five minutes flat . . . and yet can't find your G-spot? Location! Location! Location! That's all there is to say about the G-spot, really.

*

A man can calculate the total surface area of every room in your house, determine the exact mile-to-the-gallon ratio of a five-hour trip to the South of France and effortlessly locate the remote fishing village that's not even on a map – yet he can't find your clitoris? No, the truth is he just can't be bothered to find it.

*

When there's no foreplay you tell yourself to at least try for an orgasm – but then you give up the idea eventually as a waste of vaginal muscle.

*

It's good to be considerate, but not too considerate. I know a woman who faked orgasms because she didn't want to be impolite.

Oral Sex

Women have always found cunnilingus to be a good opening-courting gambit.

*

A perfect man is one who rests on his orals.

*

The Broad's Prayer – Give us this day our daily head . . .

*

Women don't want a man who performs his bit of perfunctory cunnilingus only for the penis payback – the erotic IOU that it implies.

*

Half-hearted cunnilingus is like a cow chewing methodically upon a bale of hay.

*

Beware lactose-intolerant, anally retentive vegans. He'll say he can't go down on you because he's vegetarian.

*

On the other hand . . .

If God had meant women to give blowjobs, she wouldn't have given us teeth.

*

If you were a bloke, would you put it in a mouth where there are *teeth*? The teeth of a female who's been discriminated against for centuries?

*

Men only like blowjobs because they know we can't talk with our mouths full . . .

*

Men think eating is not cheating. They see extramarital fellatio as nothing more than a parking infringement on the male moral rap sheet.

When a husband tells you, à la Bill Clinton, that eating is not cheating, reply, 'I know. That's why I only let the tennis coach go down on me! We didn't have sex. He merely yodelled up my canyon of love.'

How to get out of fellatio

Tell him that you can't swallow because you're trying to lose weight, you know, after the baby . . . Just don't mention that the child is, like, *seven*.

*

Tell him that your mother said never to put anything in your mouth which hasn't been peeled.

*

Just say to the guy that he's *so* big, it's making you gag. And when you gag, you always get the urge to *bite down*. (And if he swallows that, he'll swallow anything. Unlike you.)

*

Change his diet. Pineapple, apparently, will turn him into a sperm liqueur. Although, if God were a woman, sperm would taste like zabaglione in the first place.

Celibacy

Who needs a real man? Not when sex with Hugh Jackman is only the flick of a light switch away. You've got so many Rampant Rabbit vibrators they need their own warren.

*

Sex with Brad Pitt is amazing, you marvel when you wake in the morning . . . But how much more amazing it would be if he had actually been with you at the time.

*

There is a lot to be said for celibacy and most of it begins with 'Why ME?' When it comes to the sex war, you seem to have declared yourself a conscientious objector. Hence your dates of late in an internet chat room, typing one-handed and, on one occasion, with your *nose*.

*

If you're ever called upon to give a sex talk, you'll be lecturing from *notes*. Your clitoris has taken to sending the odd sexual SOS along the lines of 'Remember me?' If it weren't for Mrs Palm and her five daughters (although the two elder daughters usually suffice, with the other three fighting over the VCR), you would have dried up completely.

*

Reclusive Trappist yogis living in caves or even perhaps the Pope could ring you up for tips on celibacy.

*

You're so famished for bodily contact you're occasionally tempted to give yourself a strip search.

*

If it weren't for bra fittings at Marks and Spencer, you wouldn't have any sex life at all.

*

Women need sex. With no prospect of consummation, your blood pressure reaches thermonuclear levels. You're masturbating so much you need terry towelling sweatbands on your wrists. You have the most exercised right hand in human history. There hasn't been digital action like it since Proust wrote all seven volumes, longhand. You've worn off a fingerprint. But look on the bright side, you can commit the perfect crime now.

*

Celibacy can turn you into the kind of deranged woman who hatches abandoned bird's eggs in her bra.

*

You'll be reading the Kama Sutra for One.

*

It's been so long since you got laid, if you get killed in a car accident nobody will be able to identify your body.

*

Try to put a positive spin on things – you're only two people short of a threesome. (Even a dickhead man is better than *no* man. And *one* man is never quite as fulfilling as *two*.)

*

There are worse things than celibacy . . . like hepatitis and death.

*

Your only erogenous zone will be the second shelf of the cupboard where you keep the chocolate bars.

*

If you allow yourself to get too carnally malnourished you'll get aroused glancing at that picture of Paul Newman on the salad dressing.

*

You'll feel you're starring in a TV programme called *America's Least Wanted*. The Metropolitan Police will put out a chastity alert: **NOT** WANTED, DEAD OR ALIVE.

*

'Where dere comes no beau, de cobwebs grow.' In other words, don't let your diaphragm grow lichen.

*

Stay celibate for too long and you start to deduce that you possess the sexual magnetism of a half-thawed rissole.

*

How can you ever join the Mile High Club, when you're flying right under every man's romantic radar?

*

It only hits you when you order mussels from the 24-hour room service menu that you've been celibate for too long. As you prise them free from their shells with your tongue, you realize that even your meal is getting more action than you are. If you weren't so depressed you would make puns along the lines of having finally pulled a mussel. Is it any wonder that your libido is the size of Paraguay?

*

She who hesitates is celibate.

*

Chastity is curable if caught early enough.

*

If you don't have sex soon you'll end up with a Barbie stump. That little bit of moulded plastic between the legs of a Barbie doll. That'll be you. You'll heal over.

*

You convince yourself that you have no time for men. You are, after all, a very busy woman . . . you have a vibrator to take in for its, 1,000-mile service.

*

But surely, woman cannot live by vibrator alone? Your needs are melting you from sigh to thigh. Your muff's in a huff.

*

It's much easier being a bloke. Wrinkles and grey hair add character. He can eat lick an ice cream without every man in the vicinity imagining him naked. He doesn't have to commit suicide if someone turns up at a party wearing an identical outfit to his. He never has to shave below his epiglottis. He doesn't care if nobody notices his new haircut. Nor do hair-dressers charge him double for it. His phone conversations take thirty seconds, tops. Car mechanics tell him the truth. He's able to open his own jam jars. Four pairs of shoes are adequate for his whole life! And men are always in the mood. But with the right man *you*'d always be in the mood too . . .

Lust

Just because a woman can hide the primal engorgement of her libidinous organ, it doesn't mean she doesn't want to discover the supple hydraulics of his manhood *right now*.

*

When you meet a new man you lecture yourself to stay grounded. But there's another voice in your head. And what it says is 'Show me a woman with both feet planted firmly on the ground – and I'll show you a girl who can't get her knickers off.'

*

Instead of agonizing about meeting the right man, you should be making sure you've had enough wrong ones.

*

Mothers always say that one day you'll meet your Mr Right. Mind you, they also told us not to swim when we had our periods. Is there really a Mr Right? Or just a Mr Kinda OK and a couple of Everyone-Else-Has-Gone-Home-So-You'll-Have-to-Dos?

*

Liberated, hip, post-feminist? Or amoral slut? Defend your answer.

*

How can you be intimate with a strange man? Who the hell are you all of a sudden? Blanche DuBois?

*

Sexual hypocrisy is innate in the language. A man who is sexually active is a 'love god', a 'stud muffin', a 'Romeo', a 'Lothario'. A woman with the same sexual appetites as a man is a slut, a tart, a tramp, a whore. Men still expect women to be so virginal.

Man: 'Am I the first man to make love to you?'
Woman: 'Of course . . . I don't know why you men keep asking the same silly question!'

*

A girl needs a lotta experience to bonk like a virgin, lemme tell you.

*

Society allows women to feel their oats, but not sow them. But wait too long and we're criticized for going to seed.

*

A woman should sow enough oats to feed a large continent. You can always make a clean sweep of your dirty mind later on.

*

Forget your chequered past, what you need is a chequered *present*.

*

Sex with the right man is a beautiful and moving and lovely thing . . . Sex with a stranger on a train in the dead of night is even better.

*

Why should your portable PC be on more laps than you are?

*

A girl's only guilt complex should be not having enough gold in her rings.

*

You're just having a brief dabble in philanthropy. *Amorous* philanthropy.

*

Life's too short to be subtle. Why not wear your pussy on your sleeve?

*

Don't be a clit-tease. It's time to put your vagina where your mouth is, so to speak.

*

When it comes to lust, there's only one way to stop getting your knickers in a knot. Take them off.

*

Lust at first sight is quite a labour-saving device.

*

Are you moist with excitement? Does he give you a wide-on? Is your tongue hanging so far out of your head, his shag pile gets a free shampoo?

Then why not just give in to raw, uncomplicated desire? Why shouldn't women be guilty of acute lust in the first degree? You've been a good girl all your life and what good has it done you? Even your cat has forsaken you and taken up with the cardiofunk instructress in the flat downstairs. As for your sex life? You're practically *Amish*. Give you a white cap and a covered wagon and you'll be threshing wheat and churning butter in no time.

*

Men are always praised for 'getting in touch' with their 'feminine side'. Well, why can't we get in touch our *masculine side*?

*

If God hadn't meant us to hunt men, he wouldn't have given us Wonderbras.

*

If a man has prime pectoral real estate, it doesn't mean that he's out of your league. Why can't your eyes be bigger than your vagina?

*

The exquisite sight of a man standing there in his skimpy Calvin Kleins will turn you into a vegetative state. The only reaction he'll get out of you now will be photosynthesis.

*

There's only one thing you need to say. Let's go and slip into something more comfortable – like each other . . .

Why a man plays hard to get

When you want to sleep with a man who is wearing a 'Do Not Disturb' sign on his Y-fronts, if he's a sex object who objects to sex, simply say to him, 'Stay over. We can just sleep. I promise nothing will happen. I won't touch you.' It's what men always say. Then *he* can see what it's like to wake with the imprint of an erect clitoris in the small of his back.

Lusting after the wrong man

Lust is celibacy's banana skin. Occasionally you slip, OK?

*

Some men have sex appeal which is so deadly it should be registered at Police Headquarters as a lethal weapon.

*

You know he's not the right man for you, but it's a hard concept to explain to your libido, which is like a crazed animal hurling itself against the bars of its cage. There's so much electricity between you, it could be privatized.

*

It's then that the final G-string of restraint slips nonchalantly to the floor.

*

The next thing you know, your teeth are colliding in mid-air with the sort of passion that will require months of periodontal work. It's the kind of sex that won't let you stop thinking about it afterwards in full Technicolor detail. It will be vaginal déjà vu. For weeks. You'll feel sorry for all the women who will never know what it's like having him take his warm mouth to you.

*

If you're having an affair, don't tell. The definition of a secret is something your girlfriends tell everyone not to tell anyone.

*

If your husband is having an affair, why shouldn't you? The mood of a middle-aged, first-time adulteress is one of enchanted contentment, enhanced by the anticipation of there being more where that came from. If there's one thing a 25-year-old can do, it's more. There's nothing else to do but give the guy a horizontal ovation.

*

But do remember, promiscuity is not feminism. Of course men are for 'free love' as they don't have to pay for it. Some men are just laughing all the way to the sperm bank.

Male Chauvinists

I wish male chauvinists really *were* like pigs. A pig's penis is in the shape of a corkscrew. What a biological advantage! You could have sex and then open the bottle of wine afterwards. Followed up by a bacon sandwich.

*

Not all men fancy eighteen-year-olds . . . Some fancy sixteen-year-olds.

*

But then again, there is Prince Charles. Even though I'm a republican, I've loved him ever since he gave up a supermodel for a much older woman. Actually, I've loved him ever since he wanted to be a tampon. Although it does sum up his entire life – always in the right place at the wrong time.

Contraception

There is only one 100 per cent safe oral contraceptive. The word 'No' . . . Unless you're with Mike Tyson or Roman Polanski.

*

A man will *not* withdraw in time. Do you know what they call people who use the rhythm method? Parents. Copulation means population.

Tips

Beware disease: in New York there's a bar called Simplex . . . short for herpes simplex. This can really take the anxiety out of dating – but his enthusiasm will be catching . . . Literally.

*

If a patron tells you about his 'personal growth', he isn't talking about Scientology or astrology. It's enough to make you only want to have relationships with Franciscan monks. And even then you'll want to cover yourself in neck-to-knee spermicide, wear six cervical caps and use a full-length condom. And that's just for *phone sex*.

*

Crotch lice are nature's way of promoting monogamy.

*

Don't over-analyse sex. If done right, the woman shouldn't be analysing anything 'cause she'll be in a coma of sexual stupefaction. She'll be a coma-sexual.

*

Lesbianism   If you give up on men, try tits and clits. Hey, if you can't beat 'em, lick 'em.

*

If you casually mention, while trying to insert an earring, that you're having trouble finding the hole, and he replies, 'I bet you haven't said *that* for a while. At least not since childbirth!' reconsider your options. You'll never be able to teach such a man that a closed mouth gathers no feet.

*

Never sleep with a man for money. It's not that you're a 'fallen woman'. You've just lost your balance momentarily – your *bank* balance. But prostitution is never a good idea as you leave yourself open to demeaning comments from clients. As you count out the money on the bedside table, you'll chide, 'What? No tip?'

And he may reply, 'Yeah! Get some liposuction.'

*

Sex is the best, most exciting experience in the entire world . . . although have you tried sky-diving, scuba, hot air ballooning, bungee jumping, Billy Connolly concerts, Woody Allen films (full of wry observations like this one) and shoe shopping in the sales?

*

Experts say women eat chocolate in lieu of sex. The truth is women have sex in lieu of chocolate. Buy a Mars bar. (Also insertable, according to the police who arrested Marianne Faithful naked with Mick Jagger.)

CHAPTER 3

Love

Love is complicated. Even Einstein never managed to explain it.

*

Some people don't believe in love at first sight. Some don't believe in love at *second* sight. Love's arrow can be about as accurate as Bush's bombs on Baghdad.

*

If you're sceptical about love at first sight . . . make him walk by again.

*

But don't mistake lust for love. The trouble with the language of love is that orgasms tend to do all the talking. There's nothing to say but 'oh' and 'yes' and 'take me now' and 'mmmmmm' as you finally surrender, blissfully, to each other. 'Hormonal Houston. We have lift-off . . . We're going warp factor ten to Planet Passion.'

*

But there's more to love than an all-night performance and a well-read penis.

*

How do you know you're in love? Look in the mirror. Do you have that jaundiced, ill look which means you have either just eaten a bad oyster or you're coming down with the flu? Well, then you could be truly, madly, deeply in love.

*

You want to use really insipid pet names in public. You want to talk to each other in totally irritating baby voices. You want people to roll their eyes whenever you're around. Because seeing two people so in love, so united in mutual adoration, makes everyone else experience something they've never felt before – nausea to the point of projectile vomiting. New lovers really should have a minimum isolation period of, say, six months so as not to nauseate everyone they meet. 'Um, can I get you something? A beer? A glass of wine? *A psychiatrist, maybe?*'

*

Falling in love is like going to the doctor and being told that you need to put *on* weight.

*

You'll feel so high above cloud ten you won't even be able to see it. When he kisses your neck, you'll give a swoon worthy of a Beatles concert circa '66.

*

You'll feel so elated that you keep expecting air-traffic controllers to ask you to relay your position – which, at this precise moment, could possibly be on the middle shelf of the supply cupboard at work, or on the bonnet of his car in the upside-down-lotus penetration position.

*

When you fall in love you have both feet planted firmly in the air.

*

Love is just something to do when you can't go shoe shopping. Otherwise you could end up with more pairs of shoes than the entire cast of *Riverdance*.

*

Yes, it could be love . . . but then again it could be a chemical imbalance.

What men and women want

What *you* think of as love may be nothing more than MSB – Maximum Sperm Build-up.

*

Men know that money can't buy love, but it can definitely rent it by the hour.

*

For some men, a lasting relationship is based on nothing more than a common interest – him.

*

You may think he's in love. But the only person with whom he's capable of having a passionate love affair is himself. It's a love story to rival all love stories. They should make a film out of it. Put it this way: when he comes, he calls out his own name.

*

Women want a love affair which is so romantic it should be in black and white.

*

Women long to find a man who is romantic – you know . . . the type who talks to you after sex.

Falling in love with the wrong person

Life is full of mortifying moments. Peeing in a train toilet, when the door is suddenly opened by a man and you're *hovering*. Scales which speak your weight. Asking a friend when the baby's due – and she replies that she's not pregnant. Eating bananas in front of blokes. Discovering, during the over-the-head thigh exercises in your mixed Pilates class, that there's a hole in the crotch of your leotard. All these things are blush-inducing, but nothing compared to the embarrassment level of realizing you've been used by a man. When you're attracted to the wrong person, it means your hormones are in a bad neighbourhood and it's best not to venture in there alone. You're on the edge of an emotional precipice. Just don't take a giant leap forward. Does the word 'splat' mean anything to you?

*

You can say no to love . . . but sometimes it won't listen.

*

Fall in love with the wrong man and you could end up having a His and Hers Honeymoon. *His* in the remand section of prison, and *Hers* working two jobs to post his bail.

*

Love should be classified as a Class A addiction. If love is a drug, you're the all-night chemist. You need a Nicorette for love. A boyfriend-ette. If you fall in love with a man who is married or a major criminal – get thee to Romance Rehab.

*

Yet despite everything, you still worship the water he walks on.

*

Whenever you see his chocolate eyes and ready smile, you are suddenly wearing all your yearnings and desires on the outside, like the suckers of an octopus.

*

You won't be able to trust yourself to stay away from the man. You'll have to put out a restraining order on yourself. You will have to have yourself followed by a private eye to prevent you from doing dumb-ass things like getting back with the bastard.

Falling out of love

(Otherwise known as – Prawn Cocktails for Two at the Last Chance Saloon)

A jolt of misery will surge through you as you realize you've been labouring under a delusion. You'll need to join the Labouring under a Delusion Union.

*

You didn't *fall* in love, you *stepped* in – and now it's time to wipe him off your shoes.

*

Unrequited love – the safest form of sex. Stop worshipping the ground his head is in.

*

Otherwise the United Nations will declare your love life a disaster area.

*

Tell him that you'll always love *him*. It's just his life philosophy, pseudo-male feminism, rotten, ratfink, dirty-dingo lying and dress sense you can't tolerate.

*

Still, you'll always cherish the initial misconceptions you had about him – the two-faced ratbag.

*

Breaking up is a romantic 999. Give up chocolate. You'll miss the chocolate so much, you won't miss him.

*

When you've been addicted, there are bound to be withdrawal symptoms. Although in time you will get better. Soon, *whole seconds* will elapse where you won't think of him.

*

Yes, it was love at first sight . . . But then you took a second and third look. It's as if you were wearing a sign on your heart which read '*In case of emergency, break*'.

*

Who would have thought the light of your life would turn out to be such a bad match?

*

Think of him as toxic waste. In other words – *dump him*.

*

If all the poetry goes out of a relationship, then it's prose. Bad prose. Or worse – Jeffrey Archer. In other words – Prose-ac.

*

When he asks you, 'What's up?' just reply, 'The warranty on our love affair.'

*

You've being tutored by Dr Love – but on a Dr Kevorkian fellowship.

Reality

Love is hormonal hives. Curable only with a dose of common bloody sense.

*

Love is a foolish longing for life without mortgages and dentists. Romance is love without real life attached. What women need is equality, not romance. Treat us as equals, not sequels.

*

Yes, love keeps you warm . . . but so does a goosedown duvet.

*

A woman needs a man like . . . an Eskimo needs a lawn-mower. Learn to stand on your own two stilettos.

Survival tips

Never move in a man you've just met. You should at least have things in your *fridge* that have been around longer than he has.

*

Love is curable in a way that, say, a head-on collision with a petrol tanker is not. You will eventually get over him. While it's true that it once took me two years to get over a bloke I'd never met – he was David Cassidy of *The Partridge Family* and I was pre-pubescent – I did ultimately recover.

*

If you ever fall in love again, try to wipe it off your shoe before you walk it all over the carpet. It's such a messy business.

*

There's only one thing worse than being in love. Being out of it.

*

Love may be blind, but marriage is a real eye-opener.

CHAPTER 4

Commitment

Most men like being footloose and fiancée-free. They believe in life, liberty and the happiness of pursuit.

*

Women want to be head over heels in love. Most men just want the heels over the head bit.

*

Women want to talk in the plural – 'we'll do this' and 'we did that'. We want the comfort of being number one on someone's speed dial. To be cherished. To have someone who can do the harmony line on 'I Got You Babe'. To laugh at our jokes. Damn it, a girl just can't kiss her own upper eyelids. But while women want to make a Declaration of Dependence, most men tend to approach commitment like a naked guy approaches a barbed-wire fence.

*

You've made your bed and now all you want to do is lie in it – *with him*. But most men don't even masturbate over the same fantasy figure two nights in a row, in case she gets attached.

*

During your twenties, you think you've developed tinnitus, but it's just the endless ringing of wedding bells as all your friends get hitched. This is the time when a boyfriend gets increasingly nervous. He'll begin to think that all women are husband-hunters, equipped with everything bar a net and a tranquillizer dart.

*

To marry or not to marry – this is the question. A woman's thinking, we've lived together, bought a microwave and shared a genital infection. Marriage is surely the next logical step? But what the man's thinking is, should love be logical? Marriage is a natural progression – yes – but *forty to fifty years of it*? From honeymoon to tomb? Forty to fifty years of looking at the Cheesy Wotsits and chips stuck in her fillings every time she laughs. Is this really love's greatest manifestation?

*

Men think of themselves as a fine vintage and try to persuade you that a good wine takes the longest to mature. Women think that by thirty, it's decanting stage.

*

Some men are so commitment-phobic, it's amazing that they can even commit to a wine.

Waiter: 'Red or white?'

Man: 'Um . . . white, thanks.'

Woman: 'Subject, of course, to his indecision. He can't commit to a wine. As far as he's concerned, the word "commit" should only be used next to the word "murder" . . . which describes marriage, apparently.'

*

A woman knows that it's natural to get all tied up in knots about tying the knot. But whatever your joint emotional misgivings, she's sure you can work them out . . . The man is thinking, why is it that people are always using the word 'work' next to the word 'marriage'? Oil rigs you work on. Key accounts. Yachts, as a deckhand. But a relationship should be a retreat from all the things you work on.

*

For most men, love is just a four-letter word . . . Ask him if he loves you and the most articulate man on the planet will suddenly take on the speech patterns of an android from *Robots from Planet Bastard*.

*

Ask a man if he loves you and he'll become so enigmatic he'll be harder to read than advanced trigonometry.

*

As he surveys you with all the enthusiasm one gives an approaching traffic warden, you will feel bewildered. It's not like you're asking him to slay a dragon or pull a sword out of a stone. All you're asking is that he uses the L word. It's not the sort of question you have to swot for.

*

Mention the L word and he'll go out to buy a packet of cigarettes . . . and won't come back for two years. When he finally walks back in the door, just look at him and say, coolly 'Didn't they have your brand?' Then introduce him to your new boyfriend.

*

Better to find out he's a commitment-phobe *now* than on the day he leaves you standing at the altar. The best way to get rid of cockroaches is to tell them you want a long-term relationship. (Turn on the kitchen light suddenly and see if he makes an instinctive dash to get under the fridge.)

*

Jilting a woman at the altar is an act that puts a man on a par with a puppy vivisectionist. From then on, he'll be known as the 'Wedding Reneger'. Churches will burst into flames at his approach.

Procreation

It's hard enough to get a man to commit to calling you 'baby', let alone to having any. The question is: how does a clucky woman go about finding a man who wants to have children? Perfume ads are full of promises of romantic attraction. Obsession says, 'I'm a fun-loving babe.' Allure says, 'You'll have to buy me an expensive dinner first.' What we need is a perfume which says, 'Fabulously Shagable Sex Goddess Who Wants You to Father Her Children, and I'm *Ovulating Now*.'

*

Who would have thought it would be so hard locating a sperm happy to get egg all over its face?

*

Some decisions can be put off hundreds of times until they slip your mind. When it comes to commitment to babies, most men are so indecisive they should consider joining Procrastinators Anonymous – except he'll keep postponing the appointment.

*

When you're waiting for a man to commit, you feel as though your destiny has been rerouted to one of those call centres in

India where you listen to mangled versions of all your old favourites. *'Your call is important to us, but we're putting you on hold for the rest of your natural life.'*

*

Don't wait too long for a man to rise to the occasion, procreation-wise. You don't want to become a granny test-tube mum.

*

Most blokes could hold workshops on non-occasion-rising.

*

Your only commitment will be to an institution for the criminally insane for ever thinking you wanted to marry a commitment-phobic man like *him*.

CHAPTER 5

Marriage

The general consensus is that everybody should marry. It's natural. Unless you've got a very good excuse: you know, that you're a lesbian or a eunuch or are so visually challenged that you need to get your mirrors insured.

And yet, marriage statistics are currently lower than Britney Spears' bikini line. And I'm sure it's women who are getting PMT – Pre-Monogamy Tension.

*

Marriage suits men much more than women. Married men live longer than single men, and have less heart disease and fewer mental problems, whereas single women live longer than married women and have less heart disease and fewer mental problems.

*

The hideous-habit ratio between spouses is about 100:1 in the man's favour. They shed more nose hair than a moulting Labrador. *Drain-clogging* amounts of nose hair. They dribble pee on the porcelain . . . Post-Urinal Drip Syndrome. They leave matchsticks covered in earwax on the coffee table and clip toenails during foreplay.

*

In truth, love prepares you for marriage the way needlepoint prepares you for round-the-world solo yachting.

*

I can't believe that extreme sports enthusiasts, otherwise

known as organ donors, haven't taken up marriage and motherhood as the ultimate risk-taking thrill.

*

Matrimony would be easier if you could be strapped into a marriage simulator to experience the terrors and exhilaration: to see if you have what it takes. So, fasten your psychological seat belt for a bumpy ride . . .

Why marry, when you could just lease?

Female emancipation is one thing – but dying all alone in the bath and only being discovered because of an Indian summer and a fly swarm is quite another.

*

Marriage may be an open prison. But being single? That is solitary confinement.

*

A woman gets married to avoid the horror of having to hastily organize another girls' night out on Valentine's Day so that she won't be tempted to kill herself.

*

Marriage does have its good points. What a relief not to have to get naked in front of a stranger ever, ever again. Not to have to bikini wax every five seconds. Or lie on your side to make your breasts look bigger. The very thought of having a husband is relaxing – like looking at tropical fish.

*

In England one has to get hitched to prevent hypothermia. It's either that or thermal tampons.

*

Besides, it's true love. You'd do anything for him . . . Well, anything which doesn't involve sex-change operations in Thailand.

*

Which is why, when a woman hits 25, she declares open season on bridegrooms and begins the hunt for Mr Right.

*

Mr Right? Who said anything about *Mr*? She's not waiting for Mr Right but Sir, Lord . . . *Marquis* Right, at the very least!

*

But panic quickly sets in. These days if your skin's cleared up, you're too old to marry. Men are walking down the aisle with a foetus in a veil.

*

If only men would understand how simple the marital equation really is. Basically, happy wife = happy life.

PMT –
Pre-Monogamy Tension
(Reasons not to marry)

There are three billion other men in the world you're yet to see naked.

*

You have a great job, a great boss . . . a fully charged vibrator, a car that rear-demists and a washing machine that only floods the kitchen two or three times a month. What the hell do you need a husband for?

*

Marriage is a lot like root canal surgery – only not as restful.

*

The worst aspect of matrimony is that the secret of wedded bliss is such a well-kept bloody secret.

*

If your boyfriend proposes with 'Let's just do it. For better or worse,' ask him to clarify exactly how much worse. Is he going to start flossing his teeth in bed?

*

Marriage is romance's prophylactic. Do you really want to become a fellatio refusenik? To make love to a man out of duty? OK, the sex is good now, but what if your orgasm warranty expires?

*

All your life you've found it hard to avoid temptation. Soon it will be impossible to *find* any.

*

We're the first generation of wives who've had a lot of sex before marriage. Been there, licked that. We know what we're missing . . . Make sure you tell your single years how much you love them.

*

Britain has the highest divorce rate in Europe. Why not save time and money and just marry a divorce lawyer. So quick, so easy. A drive-through McMarriage – 'Till divorce do us part.'

*

A healthy relationship is all about being honest with each other . . . Now, if you can *pretend* to be honest with each other, you'll have a very happy union.

*

Marriage can make a woman feel she's lost her individuality. 'I used to be wild! I used to be interesting! I've lost my identity. You've stolen it from me!' You may need to go along to a police line-up and see if you can make an ID.

*

Some women become so dependent during their marriage, they wake in the mornings and say, 'So, how am I going to feel today?' If she was Frank Sinatra, she'd be singing, 'I did it *his* way.'

*

Men and women have different neural circuitry. While women ponder Life's Great Questions – Am I happy? Is my marriage working? Am I a good mother? – the man is thinking, have I got time to get laid and tune the carburettor before kick-off?

*

Latest British stats reveal that 80 per cent of women are now dubious about marriage. Hey, why buy the whole pig just to get a little sausage?

Weddings

A white wedding is a fairytale wedding all right. *Scripted by the Brothers Grimm.*

*

You stare in disbelief at the meringue dress which you've drunk skimmed water for four weeks to fit into. (The tradition of wearing white at weddings doesn't seem to have been dented by the fact that the bride holds the girls' night out record for the shortest amount of time between meeting someone and shagging him – nine minutes.) If the bride is wearing white, does she need to go to Formal Wear to hire a hymen?

*

Wedding presents Why is it that normal, sophisticated couples, collectors of art deco, subscribers to interior design magazines, suddenly feel an overwhelming urge to purchase crockery bullocks pulling glow-in-the-dark sleighs or tartan eggcups? But . . . whatever presents you give, make sure they're plastic, as the happy couple will be chucking them at each other in no time.

*

At the rehearsal dinner, if you find yourself pondering whether or not it would be a serious breach of wedding etiquette to snog, marry and have children with one of the guests, then call the wedding off.

*

Some couples only get married for the property portfolio. They should make their wedding vows in Real Estate

Agencies. 'To have and to sharehold. To honour and repay. Till repayments do us part.'

*

Pre-nuptial agreement: 'With my body I thee honour, all that I am I give to thee, all that I have I protect with a watertight legal document in case you ever try to get your greedy little mitts on it.' I mean, even if you *are* only marrying him for his money it's just so . . . unromantic!

Gay Hubby

In Sydney there's a man shortage. All the men are married or gay. Or married *and* gay. So, how to tell before it's too late that the man you love would prefer a Ken and Ken kind of situation? Or, as the English would say – how to tell if your fiancé is a middle-order batsperson *for the other side*? If the sex is like being ravaged by a tree sloth, then there's a pretty good chance that your fiancé has effete of clay. He's sailing up the windward passage. He leaves no buttock unturned. He drinks at the Bun Boy Bar in the Hot Cock Tavern and dines exclusively at the Rim Café. Didn't wearing the bridesmaid's dress to the wedding rehearsal kind of give you a clue? Put it this way, if sex has been a game of Orifice Roulette, it's *not* just because his aim is off.

Multiple Marriages

(Bridesmaid Revisited)

Some wives become experts in animal husbandry. (She's had seven husbands, all of them animals.) To be a successful wife you definitely need a degree in animal behavioural psychology.

*

A 'bigamist' is not a large Italian fog. It's just something that doubles a man's chances of having to take out the garbage and change the light bulbs.

The Honeymoon

(The mourning after the knot before)

The cloud nine, euphoric feeling will pass . . . maybe even by the first morning of your honeymoon. A honeymoon is supposed to be a time of orgiastic groping, serial bonking, champagne saturation and endless oral sexual gratification . . . and that's just on the plane. You're expecting to join the Mile High Club as soon as they switch on the 'You May Now Unfasten Your Pants' sign. But, in reality, you will have your first fight at the airport. On the customs declaration form you fill in on your fold-down tray table, for '*Marital Status*', you'll write with a shaky wrist, '*Disastrous*'.

*

One hour into your tropical island honeymoon and sun-lounger hostilities will probably be rivalling those of two Balkan republics. By the end of the honeymoon you could easily be doing the old goodbye and good riddance, 'marriage takes its toll so please pay at the booth' speech.

Altar egos — the reality

Wedding ceremonies should only be performed at Lourdes, because it obviously takes a miracle to make a marriage work.

*

Most marriages break up for religious reasons. He thinks he's a god and, well, she just doesn't. (Basically he should have asked for his *own* hand in marriage.)

*

All husbands think they're gods. If only their wives weren't atheists.

*

A bad marriage will bring religion into your life. Now you really will know what it's like to be in hell.

*

Married life is like playing charades when sober.

*

In the midst of life . . . we are in marriage.

*

Sure, you wanted to tie the marital knot – you just didn't realize it would be around your neck.

*

Husbands are novocaine for the soul.

*

Marriage is just something you do when you're too tired for sex. If you're wearing flannelette pyjamas to bed, what does that tell you? And it's not that you need to turn up the heating.

*

Marriage is nature's way of promoting masturbation.

Unhappily ever after

Don't put up with a husband who is careless in his appearance – i.e., he hasn't made one for a week. A marriage with an absentee husband is like a chicken with its head cut off. It may run around in a frantic fashion, but it's actually dead.

Marital ennui

A few years after the wedding, your marriage may take on the weighty, soft-boned weariness of anaesthetic. Your husband's feelings seem to fade in and out like a wartime broadcast. There you huddle, twiddling dials, desperately trying to pick up a signal: 'Receiving, over and out.' But most men are not good at communication. In that marital desert you become an emotional camel, able to survive for days on one kind word.

Communication

A wife often feels that her small intestine communicates with her more often than her husband.

*

In marriage you get the old Trappist monk treatment. If he does speak to you over breakfast, he'll be excessively polite. 'Please, after *you*.' 'No, no, I *insist*.' 'Would it be too much trouble removing your knife from my back?'

*

You have a love-hate relationship. You love him and he hates you.

*

All I can say about a bad marriage is that time passes . . . like kidney stones.

*

A 'career and family juggler' does tend to drop things – usually her hubby.

*

Perhaps marriage should go the way of other archaic traditions, like human sacrifice – which, interestingly enough, also takes place on an altar.

*

I couldn't ask for a better husband . . . much as I'd bloody well like to.

*

You may be happily married . . . but apparently your husband isn't.

*

A happy marriage is like an orgasm. Half of them are faked.

*

Unhappy marriage leaves husband and wife grinding together

like teeth. The husband wears that slightly baffled 'I want-my-money-back' expression. With any luck you'll just develop marital Alzheimer's and forget how miserable you are. Or maybe you should just shout, '*Stop this marriage! I want to get off!*'

Till divorce us do part

You know it's time to divorce when you find yourself craving the peace and tranquillity of being caught in crossfire in the Gaza Strip.

*

Remember the 'for better for worse' part of your marriage vows? Well, if it's never for better and always for worse, it's time to split.

*

Is your marriage worth saving? Make an inventory of all the things you love about him and recite them daily as a matrimonial mantra. You've got each other through chicken pox, lost luggage, the death of relatives, the guinea pig's pneumonia, flat tyres, a brush with salmonella and a bomb scare. Yes, you've been bacteria to each other, but also penicillin. You've been through so much. You didn't even kill him during flat-pack furniture erection when you were first married – grounds for homicide normally. Then there's the suntan lotion. There are parts of your back you just can't reach . . . Plus you've now finalized plans on how to landscape the garden. But what will your friends say about that? 'They're staying together for the sake of the plants, apparently'?

*

Marital argument with husband: anything you say will be distorted beyond belief and used against you.

*

Make sure your marriage counsellor isn't single. Taking advice from a single person on your marriage is like taking tap-dancing lessons from the Taliban.

*

I don't exactly know how people get the job of marriage counsellor, but I'd be very surprised if it didn't involve some kind of satanic ritual.

*

Human beings celebrate marriage before it's had a chance to happen. Usually you celebrate *after* something. Oscars happen after the movie. A christening, after the birth. Olympic medals, after the race. And do you know why people celebrate marriage before it's happened? Because there's often so little to celebrate later.

Oh, how quickly it goes from 'Till Death Do Us Part' to 'What the Hell Did I Ever See in You, You Asshole?'

*

You come to the conclusion that you *could* be happily married . . . all that's stopping you is your husband.

*

You are going to enjoy this marriage . . . even if I have to divorce you to do so.

CHAPTER 6

Domesticity

I had always wanted to be one of those superwomen who naturally assume responsibility for household DIY, balancing a chequebook with one hand and changing a light bulb with the other, then whipping up an entire gourmet meal for all the children plus their friends and any local waifs and strays, even though the larder is bare and all I have in the fridge is some thrush cream, wart medicine and half a bulb of garlic.

But once I got married and had children, I rapidly realized that 'home cooking' is just that place where a bloke thinks his woman is. As I stuffed grapes up tiny birds' bottoms, it began to vaguely cross my mind that perhaps Ms Pankhurst had tied herself to the railings for more than this.

My favourite recipe: *take one domestic goddess, roast slowly on a spit.*

To me, 'capers' are things you get up to, preferably with a recently divorced retail magnate.

*

It's not that I'm a shirkaholic. It's just that I'm convinced that historians will look back on this era as the Dark Ages Mark 2. All the women I know are ricocheting from one nervous breakdown to another, leaving a trail of feral, au-pair-reared children in their wake, juggling dinner parties and Prozac overdoses and extramarital affairs (because their workaholic husbands are too tired for sex), gushing all the time from their beds in a psychiatric unit that they'd be bored if they didn't work.

*

But stay-at-home mums are no better off. So much for that political science degree as she is now the Imelda Marcos of choux pastry. The woman who used to wax lyrical about literature, is now waxing parquet and making her own pot pourri . . . An invitation announcing a surprise party for the pet terrapin is the highlight of her social life. She's doing hospital corners on the newspaper lining of the hamster cage . . .She'd better watch out that her halo doesn't slip and choke her to death.

Become a stay-at-home mum and society hands you an eviction notice. You're suddenly a runner-up in the human race. Call yourself a housewife and men instantly dismiss you. You get seated down table at dinner parties. My advice is to call yourself a 'domestic engineer'. Or a 'highly skilled operative at the interface between culinary and residential management provision'. Or simply 'President of In-Home Pedagogy'.

As everyone knows, if motherhood was advertised in a jobs column, it would read 'Must be good at making mince interesting, finding the lost glove and the square root of the hypotenuse [most men don't even know that it's lost!]. Hours constant, time off nil, no sick pay, no holiday pay – hell, no pay.'

*

The Dunkirk evacuation would be easier to organize than a working mum getting her kids up and out of the house in the morning. Husbands say they'd like to help more around the house, only they can't multi-task. This, girls, is a biological cop-out. Can you imagine any man having any trouble multi-tasking at say, an *orgy*?

*

The enlistment of labour on a subsistence basis is now forbidden, except in one state – the holy state of matrimony.

*

I used to think that the ultimate proof of female superiority is the fact that we live longer than men. But then I realized that was just so typically male, leaving all the cleaning up to a woman.

*

And it's exhausting. One morning I was so tired, I toasted my hand with strawberry jam and placed it on my daughter's plate. Many a time, I've thrown clothes into the washing machine – with kids still in them.

*

Of course, the reason women are so crap at maths is because men are able to trick us into believing that they're doing 50 per cent of the cleaning, cooking and childcare.

*

A woman's work is never done. Not by men anyway. Sweeping a woman off her feet is the closest most men ever come to housework, besides leaving a roasting pan to soak and looking thoughtfully at the washing-up now and then.

*

The male attitude to house cleaning: no sooner do you finish than you have to do it all again, like, two lousy months later.

*

Men seem to think that a woman's wedding vows read 'To love, hoover and obey'.

*

So, are men missing the DNA structure that would enable them to find the nail clippers, the TV remote, dry-cleaned shirts, matching socks, Panadol and black bow ties – things located, *amazingly*, exactly where they've been for the past ten years? Are they genetically geared to stand in front of the open refrigerator door and gaze at the interior for hours waiting for something to materialize? To rip holes in the sides of bread packets? To blow their noses in the shower and pick them at traffic lights? To insist on driving the car – except at the end of a drunken dinner party when they suddenly announce that *you*'d better drive? Or is it just laziness and learned helplessness?

*

If he wants breakfast in bed, tell him to sleep in the kitchen.

*

The only bucket a woman should ever handle is the one with champagne in it.

*

My top housework tip: offer a husband a sexual reward for housework. He'll vacuum so thoroughly, he'll practically suck the skirting boards right off the walls.

Living together: the chief cause of breaking up

Lack of male domesticity means that living with a man is about as relaxing as amateur ovarian cyst removal. His shelves have topsoil. There's usually enough dirt under his nails to support organic farming on a commercial scale. Once you move in with a man, his arms will mysteriously atrophy whenever he's in the vicinity of the kitchen.

*

But why is it a surprise? His bachelor flat should have told you everything you needed to know. A single man's stove is so greasy it looks like another Exxon disaster. The fridge will be empty, bar a couple of beers, a Cracker Barrel cheese left unwrapped and a few petrified lumps which could once have been salami. His refrigerator is a penitentiary for food sentenced to life imprisonment. You'll find yoghurt whose expiry date reads 'When dinosaurs roamed the Earth'. You'll find chutney bottled during the reign of Elizabeth I.

*

Your average bachelor's bedroom is so rancid even the bed lice walk away with disdain. The pillows have no cases and the only beverage on offer is out-of-date juice drunk straight from the cardboard carton. His flatmates shake their knobs and make woo-woo noises as they return from a bathroom which is full of *E. coli* bacteria big enough to saddle up and ride home. A woman should demand medical benefits before entering such an unsavoury environment. And yet what do we women then do? Move him into our nice clean homes.

*

Hygiene   Most men can't turn down a bed. Anybody's. Which is why you should suggest that while he's washing his clothes, why not throw himself in with them? Left to his own devices, the average man reverts to bachelordom. But it doesn't mean you have to become his unpaid domestic servant. Tell him that the only Iron Man competitions women would like to see would involve the male of the species, some starch and a laundry basket. The trick is to pretend to be even worse at housework than he is.

Survival tips

Housework   Tell him you feel like blowing up the marital home, while chortling maniacally, 'That'll be the housework done, then!'

*

Convince him that you use your smoke alarm as a timer.

*

Tell him you don't cook. You burn. And what you don't burn, you thaw. If charred black you simply call it Cajun. (A new taste sensation – Cordon Noir.) And if it's undercooked – sushi.

*

Tell him that to you, cuisine really means 'quizz-ine' – you're never quite sure how the recipe will turn out.

*

Cooking for his parents can be more gruelling than a samurai initiation. It's a form of S&M (Sado-Mastication). Assure him that your only recipe for a dinner party is to drive over to a girlfriend's house around suppertime. Tell him that your idea of interior decorating is to line tummies with fish fingers and creamed regurgitated-from-the-can corn. When he asks why you never cook for his family, just reply it's because you don't want to go down for manslaughter.

*

Let him know early that you can't even do the gravy . . . or you'll be arrested for carrying a congealed weapon.

*

Tell him that your recipe for dinner party success is to leave get-well cards all over the mantelpiece so that people will imagine you've been too ill to cook, which is why you're ordering takeaway. (If you can't stand the heat . . . order Chinese.)

*

Do all this and he'll be domesticated in no time . . . but be careful. If your husband says he likes to help with the 'domestics', make sure he doesn't mean that he likes to *do* them. Jude Law and Robin Williams both had affairs with their nannies. Men are so lazy. They just use anything that's lying around the home.

*

If a man ever says to you that the only difference between his wife and his job is that after five years his job still sucks, simply explain that it is scientifically proven that no woman ever shot her hubby while he was vacuuming. Now *that* really is the ultimate blowjob.

CHAPTER 7

Parenthood

The only thing worse than getting your period is not getting it. A pregnancy test is the one test you can't cheat in. It's also the time you find out that when it comes to parenthood, men are about as useful, well, as a father in a delivery room.

*

It is Stone Age, what happens to women during childbirth. Completely prehistoric. As you lie with your feet up in stirrups, adoption starts to look like a very attractive alternative. If you ever had any doubt about the gender of God, you now know that he's a bloke. But the blokes are no help . . .

Insignificant other

My husband didn't want to be there at the birth. But, hey, *I* didn't want to be there! If he was there when it went in, he should be there when it comes out!

*

He's supposed to wipe your fevered brow. It's in the *Husband Handbook*. But little did I know that he was going to completely take over . . .

*

When the guru sat at the front of the birthing class and said, 'So, who's having a natural childbirth?' *all the men put their hands up.* You know what men are like with pain? They need an epidural to get their ingrown toenails cut!

*

Natural childbirth is a case of stiff upper labia. You've done drugs all your life, why stop now?

*

The cognoscenti may be big on Leboyer, but I'm an advocate of unnatural childbirth. The only natural thing about my births is that I didn't get time to bikini wax first. The only way I could be talked into childbirth again would be with a promise of daily epidurals from the moment of conception till the child reaches twenty.

*

If a man were asked to grow an alien in his belly for forty weeks, causing varicose veins, wind, amnesia and halitosis, followed by thirty-six hours of intense agony culminating in a cut from testes to anus – even James Bond would decline on the grounds that it was too damn dangerous.

*

I think of natural childbirth the way I think of natural leg amputation or appendectomy. Just aim for the 'Full-Anaesthetic-Elective-Caesarean-Wake-Me-When-It's-Over-and-the-Hairdresser's-Here' approach.

*

If the father of your child doesn't turn up to the labour ward, don't contract *pre*-natal depression (the first case known to medical science). Just realize that he's your *in*significant other and unsettle him by saying, with a smile, that the only good thing about being a woman is never having to worry about who the mother is.

Childbirth

In the labour ward, the mother's heart soars in her body. As the baby crowns she smiles a smile big enough to admit a banana sideways – while the average father is thinking footage. When he appears with a video camera trained between your legs squish his head with your knees and explain that it would have been more interesting to film the conception.

*

The only reason to have the man there at the birth is that it's the one time to get anything you've ever, ever wanted. While you're groaning and moaning and he's saying, 'Is there anything I can get you, darling?' answer, 'New car, new carpet, holiday in the Caribbean.' They're the pregnancy cravings *I* got.

*

The only other advice you need is:
1) Don't have the enema, because crapping on the man who knocked you up in the first place will be the most satisfying revenge.

2) When the doctor is sewing you up after the episiotomy, just tell him to keep on sewing. You don't want anything going in or coming out of there ever again.

The baby

The real sexist joke is that the birth is a doddle compared to what comes next – cracked nipples, constipation, mountains of haemorrhoids – Edmund Hillary couldn't scale those bastards. And it's so boring. Sometimes a mother is so bored she can see her plants engaging in photosynthesis. I once grew a yeast infection *as a change of pace*.

*

But no matter how bad it gets, you can't escape. Your bloke can nip off down the pub, but you are tethered by the tit. You are a 24-hour catering service – Meals on Heels.

*

And even when your bloke's at home he's no help. He's conveniently developed selective aural and olfactory tendencies. Even though he can still smell a baked dinner being cooked in the Outer Hebrides, he's suddenly unable to whiff a filthy nappy on the child *in his lap*. This sudden nasal congestion is only matched by his sporadic deafness. While he can hear a beer can being pulled open at an Arctic base camp, his erratic hearing means he can't detect a squealing baby in the cot *by his head*. 'Oh, sorry, love, was the baby crying?' It's learned helplessness, a special talent perfected by generations of fathers.

*

Dad (nose pinched between fingers): 'I think the baby needs changing.'
Mum: 'Yes . . . preferably for the heir to an oil fortune.'

*

Perhaps dads are so reluctant to change nappies because they can't understand why their baby sons don't just disappear into the lavatory for hours on end with a copy of *Sporting Life*.

*

Parenting manuals warn that, after the birth, some men may feel usurped, rejected and neglected. What such books should say is that men like this . . . should be strung up by their testicles immediately.

*

Wife (kissing her beautiful newborn's cheek): 'Who's Mummy's lovely baby boy?'
Husband (sulkily): '*I* am, actually."

*

The only way to get fathers involved in their babies is to explain things in terms of football or automobiles. With any luck, he'll think that 'gross motor skills' mean driving a tacky car.

*

If you want the father of your children to be involved, then invest in gadgets. While new mothers acquire the ability to discuss their baby's bowel movements long after the listener's own interest has waned, Dads become Cecil B. DeMilles, videoing every nanosecond of the child's life for the archives, then immediately viewing the footage. 'Brings back memories, doesn't it?' he'll sob.

Designer genes

Over half of all marriages end in divorce, so before having unprotected sex ask yourself, is *this* the man whose name you want your baby to see on the child maintenance cheques every month?

*

The only thing worse than taking the consequences is giving birth to one of them.

*

Unplanned pregnancy: there's a baby in my bathwater!

*

Men sow wild oats while praying for a crop failure.

*

Most men test positive to allergies to nappies, Lego, broken sleep, having little gates all over the house and only buying food which harmonizes with animated cooking utensils on daytime TV. 'My fridge is too small,' he'll say. 'I've got nowhere to put those awful finger paintings. I told you not to fall pregnant.'

But you didn't 'fall' pregnant. You were bloody well pushed.

*

It doesn't require a mathematical genius to work out that it takes two to make a baby. It's a foetal attraction.

*

What's the difference between a pregnant woman and a light bulb? You can unscrew a light bulb.

*

A man should have a bumper sticker on his penis saying, 'Caution: Baby on Board'.

*

Be warned – even older men can still fire live ammunition. He may tell you that you're his sexual swan song, but there could be a cygnature tune.

*

And there really is nothing more pathetic than a geriatric father taking a nap at the same time as his teething toddler: one in a nappy and one in incontinence pants.

*

On becoming a father: at least most men are programmed to the baby's schedule – up all night, drinking.

*

Many blokes think Ovulation is a warm milk drink before beddy-byes.

*

Some men think a paternity suit is the latest look in men's leisurewear.

*

Some fathers chicken out of their obligation to their eggs.

*

What a sham. What a Havisham. But Miss Havisham was better off. At least she wasn't up the duff when he ditched her. Even Mary and Joseph had a stable relationship.

Custody

The reason most mums get custody is that fathers just don't have the right qualifications; he hasn't a bloody clue how to make models of space stations using old shoeboxes, at short notice on a school night.

*

Most men only know how to look after *dogs*. The child will be cocking its leg on trees within days. Next time you see your son, he'll come to heel when called and catch a Frisbee between his teeth.

*

If the footie's on, the baby monitor will say, 'Sorry, but the father you are trying to reach is temporarily disconnected. Please try again.'

*

Leave a father alone with the kids for a weekend and he'll shove them back into the condom-vending machine for a refund.

*

Crisp jeans and spotless jumper, no doubt hand-knitted by Peruvian lesbians, is a sign he's a Gentleman Father: the type who holds forth at every opportunity about the joys of fatherhood . . . but farms his kids out to a nanny at the drop of a small turd.

Exes

An ex may state that he should be able to see his kids when *he* has time and not just when you do. If he whines, 'My access should be when it's convenient for us both,' simply reply, 'Well, it wasn't particularly convenient for me when you started shagging my best friend and moved out, now was it, you dingo-dicked bastard.'

Upper-class English men

Do you know how the upper-class bloke breaks the news of his impending fatherhood? 'Dah-ling, we're going to have a nanny!' The reason upper-class English men are so flawed as human beings is because their mothers left them with the nanny, who left them at the bottom of the garden and fed them by the clock. That was the doctrine of the baby guru Truby King. Well, not only did Truby turn out to be a New Zealander, and a man, but his whole philosophy was based on the scientific rearing of bucket-fed calves on an asylum farm. Need I say more?

Circumcision

The only possible reply to a man who insists that his son be circumcised because *he* was is 'Yeah, and they threw away the wrong part.'

Hypocrisy in the workplace

Mums must pretend to have an allergy to children. Male bosses frisk you upon arrival for finger paintings or photographs, whereas when a man with a framed baby photo on his desk takes time off for sports days he's praised for his sensitivity and well-roundedness.

*

A dad like this will soon be writing articles on the importance of quality time with one's children ... while ignoring plaintive pleas from his own offspring to come and lose at Monopoly.

*

Even though mothers butter 4,000 acres of toast, roast hundreds of flocks of lambs and herds of cows and schools of salmon; even though we run trays up to a child's room for nothing more serious than a stubbed toe; even though we unpick our kids' pee-stained shoelaces with our *teeth* – your baby's first word will be 'Dad'.

*

And when you eventually divorce him for taking all the credit but not doing any of the work, your teenagers will blame you. 'Yeah, right, I was married to a bloody saint. I'll send away for the necessary paperwork to have the bloke canonized the second I get the chance,' you want to flippantly reply – although, of course, you don't, as you don't want to psychologically scar the little poppets.

*

Dignity is a superfluous emotion for mothers. Like styling mousse for bald men.

*

Which is why you won't even break down when your teenage daughter screams, 'This divorce is all your fault. I hate you! I wish you'd just die!'

Simply have another swig of wine, take a drag on one of the cigarettes you stopped smoking ten years ago and reply, 'I'm doing my best, darling.'

CHAPTER 8

Infidelity

Fifty per cent of married people are having affairs and the other 50 per cent will no doubt be looking for one as soon as they read that statistic.

*

Husbands and wives no longer separate after dinner. No, they separate at the end of the evening to go to their respective lovers.

*

But the question on the minds of most women is, how can a husband have a midlife crisis when he's never left puberty?

*

Many men go straight from puberty to adultery.

*

But to be an adulterer, surely you have to be an actual adult first?

*

An adulterer is a bloke who helps himself because he can't help himself.

*

Boys will be boys . . . and so will a lot of octogenarian businessmen who should know better.

*

Philandering is a disease of male nymph glands. He is sexually incontinent.

*

A new invention is required. The monogamous husband. Patent pending.

*

'Devoted husband' is oxymoronic.

*

When the right man comes along, most women have the strength of character to say, 'No, thank you – I'm already married.'

*

There are always going to be things about which one can do nothing: the supermarket express checkout queue moving more slowly than the other lanes, freak asteroids . . . and husbands being unfaithful.

*

Behind every successful man is a wife . . . Under every successful man is a mistress. (Otherwise known as a mattress.)

*

Around middle age, your previously strait-laced spouse will become a heat-seeking moisture missile.

*

But if he's going to have a midlife crisis, couldn't he just, I dunno, buy an impractical car? Or cross the Channel on a homemade raft? I mean, isn't that ridiculous motorbike enough?

*

When your husband says he's leaving you for a younger woman because he 'needs more space', retort: 'Space? Well, may I suggest that you look between the ears of your pubescent princess?'

*

By the time a husband 'finds himself', there'll be nobody home.

*

To stop him getting lost, install a psychological sat nav. 'You have taken a wrong turn. Go back to your wife. Cerebral cul-de-sac.'

*

Women like a man who is in touch with his feminine side – but not on another woman.

How to tell if your husband is having an affair

Has your sex life become like trying to thread a needle with spaghetti? Is he flossing during foreplay? Is he smoking *during* sex? Does he drape his arm limply across the back of your shoulders with all the passion of a beach towel? A very good guage that your marriage is going stale is if the last time you tongue-kissed was when he'd spent too long underneath a wave in the Caribbean.

*

Is he being callous and neglectful? Paying you no attention except to put you down? Did you find a love bite on his arse which he dismissed as a tennis injury but you are praying is the bubonic plague?

*

What happened to the tender, sensuous man you married? Is the closest you get to sex now a nice pat-down from a security guard? Is your favourite sexual fantasy *a partner*? If you're so lonely you've taken to sexually harassing yourself, chances are he's become a sexual kleptomaniac.

*

Is your husband coming home four hours late? And worse – is he coming home cleaner than he went out? Does he use mouthwash before kissing you hello? These are all subtle ways to realize that you're married to a two-timing worm. In fact, the local council should issue a fumigation order immediately.

*

Is he insisting on introducing new sexual positions into your R-rated repertoire? When your inner thighs are rasping from something you're pretty sure he called the 'Rotating Helicopter', followed by the 'Full Cream' – where you found yourself flipped on top, legs closed, facing the ceiling, with your husband's hips undulating against your butt, his hands nipple-twirling and clit-tweaking – you may start getting that who's-been-sitting-in-*my*-chair-sleeping-in-*my*-bed-fucking-*my*-husband feeling.

*

Does your husband's secretary look too happy? Is she on something? . . . Your husband's face, for example?

*

It's time to say goodbye to childhood, hello to adultery.

*

You now have a serious case of Husband Uncertainty Syndrome.

*

Husband: 'I am *not* losing interest in you sexually. How can you say that?'

Wife: 'Gee, I dunno. Maybe it has something to do with the fact that during sex I looked up to notice that my husband *was in another woman's bed*!'

*

A sure sign your husband is being unfaithful: 'What's that on your penis, darling? Oh look! It's my best friend's mouth.'

Finding out

The realization that life hasn't quite turned out the way we thought it would hits us all at some time. It is prompted by many things. The kids flying the nest . . . other people's gazebo extensions. Finding your husband lying face down on your massage therapist.

When you discover your husband in bed with your best friend / the nanny / the pool boy / the hamster, etc., if you were on an airplane, it would be a 'Please return to your seats, extinguish your cigarettes and put on your life jackets' kind of moment.

*

He'll descend into snivelling. There'll be a lot of 'I didn't mean to hurt you's and 'I don't know what came over me's and 'I was obviously having some kind of breakdown's.' You would have to have a heart of stone to listen to your husband's apology for adultery – without laughing your head off.

*

You'll take to calling yourself 'the patient'. As in 'The patient has a philandering husband, but no other abnormalities.'

*

Your husband may say to you, 'How can adultery be a crime? That would make loving a crime and where's the sense in that?' This is a little like saying if you eat meat it's OK to be a cannibal.

What to do?

Obviously your marriage vows said for better for worse, but . . . not for a younger woman.

*

You can either stalk him until he becomes so freaked out he finally breaks down and moves back in. Or, of course, you can kill him.

*

The modern working mother has a lot of arduous responsibilities – birth, breastfeeding, board meetings, speech night, late homework assignments – but being civil to her husband's mistress is not one of them.

*

Christmas will be a wonderful opportunity to bond with the family – which is why your husband is bringing his girlfriend and you're thinking about bringing your hit man . . . And why you'll all be bringing food tasters.

*

Your husband walking out on you affords all the joys of getting your arm caught in the food disposal unit. Only it's much more disabling. After all, you'd eagerly give an arm and a leg to get him back.

*

One of life's great mysteries, apart from the fact that TV weathermen get a clothing allowance and still look the way they do, is why women continue to stand by their cheating husbands. I mean, *men* don't stay in a relationship when they don't think it's working. Stephen Hawking walked out on *his* marriage and the man's in a wheelchair.

*

Forgiveness   He's behaved like an animal. A man like that shouldn't be able to travel to the States without going through quarantine. But if you still love him, then the race is on. You will win back your hubby, fair and square . . . even if you have to cheat to do so.

*

Stick a sign on your man reading '*This is not an abandoned husband.*'

*

Tell him that if he so much as looks at another woman again you'll wash his eyes out with soap.

*

But be warned. If it's a friend's hubby who's bolted, be careful how much you run him down, as he may soon be reinstated. Just say, 'I never comment on my friends' husbands and I'm not going to break my rule for that two-timing clit-jockey.'

Taking the phallic cure

We swear in our marriage vows not to be led into temptation. But let's face it, most of us can find the way blindfolded.

But if your husband has been unfaithful, taking a lover is much more rejuvenating than face cream. Toyboy temptation will make you feel sexy and wanted. It will make you feel young. The question is not why are you having an affair with a Love-God, but why aren't *more* women having them? You can control your feelings for him . . . with medication.

*

Female midlife crisis is not as well documented as the male version. But around forty, the idea of infidelity will thrust itself between a woman's legs.

*

'*We apologize for this temporary loss of service. Normal devoted-wife activity will resume at the end of this unimportant midlife crisis.*'

*

It's easy to have the pants charmed off you if the elastic isn't too strong to begin with. Ping! There go those elastic morals again!!

*

Etiquette tip: exactly what *is* the correct behaviour when your husband catches you with your teeth in the fly of another man? Spontaneous combustion.

*

Generally speaking, there are four words a woman doesn't want to hear while enjoying cunnilingus. They are 'Hi, darling. I'm home.'

CHAPTER 9

Divorce

'*For sale: one husband. Has had only one careful lady owner.*'

*

Divorce is the future tense of 'Let's get married'.

*

Half of all marriages today end in divorce . . . and let's face it, more ought to.

*

Statistically, 100 per cent of divorces begin with marriage.

*

An unhappy marriage creeps up on you. Like bad underwear.

*

This means that there's a good chance you could turn into the sort of couple who indicate the happiness of your marital union by giving each other head injuries with the nearest household implement.

*

One day it will dawn on you that your husband no longer loves you. It's as obvious as a pre-1990 nose job. Your husband's love is fading away, like the end of a pop song on the radio. So, how does it go from 'Fuck me!' to 'Fuck you!'? Suddenly you're looking down at your marriage as though it's a corpse on a mortuary slab. You stare at each other blankly, like two people passing on up and down escalators.

*

Man: 'Where did our love go?'
Wife: 'To the Oxfam shop, with the rest of your stuff.'

Get the marriage annulled on the grounds that the immaturity of the husband made him incapable of giving informed consent.

Initial panic

At first you'll panic. You've been married so long your wedding certificate should be in hieroglyphics.

*

How will you cope without him? You call every gadget a 'thingy'. Your only DIY experience is in the highly technical art of whacking the crap out of any electronic device to make it work again. Thank God wine bottles now have twist tops, because even a corkscrew is probably beyond you.

*

The two worst things that can ever be said to a woman are 1) 'Yoo-hoo – hey, listen to that echo!' in the middle of oral sex. And 2) 'I don't love you any more.' Suddenly you're a romance fatality – a chalked outline in the marital stakes . . .

*

If your husband ever tries to justify leaving you by saying that you've become like brother and sister, ask him, 'Where? In Tasmania? A brother and sister who have sex and make two babies? I think that's illegal actually.'

*

When he tells you he wants a divorce you'll feel sick to your stomach. Was it something you ate? Yes – your wedding cake.

*

The shock will be immense. You have joint pension schemes. You've planted gingko bilobas. You were planning to spend your final years chasing the winter sun on a Caribbean cruise ship with a questionable cabaret. Then, one affair and hey presto. Two cars you can't sell, a vacuum cleaner which doesn't work, a custody fight over the cat and his new girl-friend moulting hair extensions all over your children in the school sports day mothers' race, in which she beats you.

*

What to say at the end of a marriage: 'It's been nice. But I really have to go and have a nervous breakdown now.'

*

You are obviously just one husband short of a very happy marriage.

The husbandectomy

Of course, more and more often now it's the wife who breaks the state of holy deadlock. For the first time in history, the majority of divorces in the West are initiated by women.

*

If anyone tells you that your marriage wasn't that bad, reply that yes, other than the infidelity, the psychological abuse, the mental torture, the shrivelled bank accounts, the domestic blindness, the emotional amnesia and the manipulation of your children, you've yet to notice any downside.

*

Man: 'You can't divorce me! On what grounds?'
Woman: 'Irreconcilable differences. We seem to have different ideas about dental hygiene. I mean, you seem to think it's OK to put another woman's genitalia into your mouth. On behalf of the Academy, we would like to offer you this award for the best fake marriage.'

*

Now that women are economically independent, we no longer have to fake a happy marriage. I can't believe it's not marriage! It smells, tastes, looks and spreads like marriage, but it just *isn't*.

Getting over him
(or I'm so miserable without him,
it's almost like he's here)

If only you could send away for the abandoned wife manual, full of handy tips for those whose husband's wedding vows said, 'From here to eternity . . . or till someone hotter comes along.'

*

Don't sit around reading one of the many self-help books entitled *Why Husbands Hate Their Wives and Leave Them and Why It's All Your Fault, You Fat, Middle-Aged Frump*, volume twenty-six. It is not your fault. Although it *is* your fault if you don't down a lot of vodka with your mates.

*

Don't go for a medal in the women's long-distance cross-bearing. Go on a girls' night out instead. Drink cocktails whose names are spiked with an innuendo you're drunk enough to find funny. Discuss male partners' anatomical details at length (or not) including width (imperative for any mothers in your midst), only to regain consciousness twenty-four hours later in the jockstrap of a spent Gladiator.

Yes, you may regret it in the morning. So sleep in.

*

A woman on the brink of a divorce is bound to drink too much and end up naked in an unfamiliar nation and with nipple jewellery. If anyone asks, 'Where is your dignity?' simply reply, 'Gee, I dunno. Maybe it got mixed in with my husband's stuff when he moved the hell out to live with his bimbo.'

*

Go to a male strip show. I have nothing against half-naked men . . . Hell, I wish I did! The nicest thing about nude male dancing is that not everything stops when the music does . . .

*

Just make sure you only get drunk with people who won't let you dance naked on a table top or do the school run topless.

*

But don't drink and drive. No police officer is going to be moved by the fact that you feel the need to keep your car with you at all times, so that it won't leave you for a younger owner. Well, no *male* officer.

*

In the mornings, you'll be so hungover you can only eat soup – everything else will be too noisy. Your head will thump so badly you'll ask the lady next door to keep her needlepoint down.

*

When traded in by their husbands, all women make a misguided lunge for the wine bottle. Next will be the peroxide bottle. Just don't get them confused.

*

You may give up eating. Or rather, eating will give up you.

*

Alternatively, you may require speed bumps in the kitchen to slow down your progress to the fridge. When heartbroken it's important not to skip a meal, even if it's four or five courses an hour.

*

You'll be angry with all men. You'll be in that 'if-you-can't-say-something-bad-about-men-then–don't-say-anything-at-all' phase. You may feel that men are perfectly agreeable and totally wonderful . . . as long as you never let them within a ten-mile radius.

*

A best friend's job is to act as a human Wonderbra – uplifting and supportive and making the dumped woman look bigger and better. (Her husband's been as supportive as a trainer bra on Dolly Parton.)

*

When your husband dumps you, turning up at his office wearing boxer shorts, a peekaboo bra, his dinner jacket and a pair of antlers on your head is probably *not* the best way to win him back.

*

It is time to master DIY. You'll learn so much . . . like the fact that as soon as your hands become coated and icky with grease, your nose will begin to itch and you'll suddenly be desperate to pee. Of course, as you're now doing your own DIY, phone calls will soon start coming through on the waffle iron and when you turn on the television, the shower will run. But it's a start, right?

*

At first you'll feel overwhelmed with new tasks. While you devoted yourself to the cooking, cleaning and child-raising, your husband has been the chequebook balancer and smoke alarm battery changer. He's the one who made sure the house insurance was up to date, the private health care paid for and the radiators bled. He's always been on hand to fix things that leaked, fumed or boiled over. He knows where the fuse box is situated and what to do when he gets there. How will you live without him? What will you do about vehicle maintenance and shifting heavy objects and Allen keys? Who is going to open the honey jars? Who's going to take all the holiday snaps and never be in them? Who's going to shine torches around in a manly way or drive to the all-night chemist at three in the morning? Just buy the one gadget you really *do* deserve – a de luxe vibrator, one that can do everything imaginable . . .

including bake fairy cakes for the school fête and complete a project on igneous rocks while unpacking the dishwasher.

*

On the positive side, you will lose weight. Your only workout will be a daily three-hour worry about where your marriage went wrong. It's a mental and emotional marathon.

*

A few months after the divorce and you'll feel you're coping. You really are. OK, you've been hiding in the rhododendrons outside his country mansion all weekend listening to his new girlfriend playing with your kids and you've been through their bins to see what they're drinking (vintage Krug) and what they're eating (lobster). But you haven't been served an injunction not to go within a ten-mile radius of their residence, so that's a step on the road to recovery, right?

*

But whine for longer than a year about how much you miss that snake-bellied, two-faced scumbag and even your pot plants will file for divorce.

Custody

Yes, he loves your children so much that he'd do absolutely anything for them – except, of course, live under the same roof as their mother.

*

Make him promise to see his kids regularly. Stress that this is not like a wedding vow. *This actually counts.*

*

And remember, he may bad-mouth you to your kids, but don't sink to his level. Just because parents are at war, it doesn't mean they should conscript their children.

Alimony, or how do I hate thee?

(Let me count the ways)

Of course, there are always two sides to every marital breakdown. Yours, and that arsehole's.

*

It'll be an amicable split. You'll both get 50 per cent of the acrimony.

*

There's no such thing as an amicable divorce, but try to have a get-together where neither of you leaves in a police car or an ambulance.

*

When meeting a soon-to-be-ex-husband, it's best not to resolve your differences with firearms.

*

Both of you made a mistake, but only one of you is going to pay for it. Just don't let it be you. Men do not fight fair in a divorce. So why should you?

*

Breaking up is hard to do – but dividing the book collection? Unbearable. Hide everything you want before the initial inventory.

*

If your ex-husband tells you he's not able to make his child maintenance payments, while lavishly supporting his new girl-friend, point out that the only job *she's* ever had was on her nose.

*

When you hear his first divorce settlement offer, reply, 'So *that's* what an oily rag smells like.' Don't sign anything until you get a lawyer to read it from covert to covert.

*

Don't phone your ex. What on earth could you say to the bas-tard that can't be said by a divorce lawyer? Besides 'Oh, honey, the proctologist called. *They found your head.*'

*

When you see a solicitor about child maintenance, he'll ask you in a routine way whether or not you have any convictions. Tell him, 'Yes. That all men are bastards.'

When the pinstriped solicitor reiterates, 'No, I mean *prior* convictions,' reply, 'Yes, that all the men I met *prior* to my husband were bastards too, I just didn't bloody well know it!'

*

You don't want to be one of those women who get nothing in the divorce. Except syphilis. You're like – '*Thanks for sharing.*'

*

There is no such thing as a good divorce. Get your lawyer to follow the paper trail, as the man you once trusted with your life has probably hidden all your joint savings. He will have arranged things with more care than a balding newscaster takes with his hair strands. *The Ex-husband. Comes in Regular, Lethal and now More Advanced Lethal!*

*

Wife to husband who is being mean with the divorce settlement: 'If you really want to torture me, ask me to renew our wedding vows.'

*

'Divorce' is an old Latin term for 'send your lawyer to a luxury resort in Bali'.

*

Everything gets shared equally . . . usually between your lawyers. Lawyers just charge a humungous amount to tell you what you already know, except they tell it to you in Latin. Divorcicularus You-Are-Screwed-Maximus or Palimony Maximum. But take heart. It probably won't come to that. Mainly because there'll be nothing to share . . . You will have thrown it all at each other weeks ago.

*

He had always been the first to put his hand in his pocket. Post-divorce he just forgets to take it out again.

*

He'll get the Wedgwood and the Royal Doulton. And you? The paper plates. He's being very fair about the separation. He's letting you keep your own toenails and internal organs.

*

When a hubby runs out on his wife, he never forgets his manners; when it comes to destitution, it's still mothers and children first.

*

What will you say to the kids? 'Sorry, but due to a downturn in our economic situation, I'm going to have to let one of you go'?

*

Your daughter will have to start wearing your hand-me-downs – while you're still wearing them. You'll be eating cereal with a fork to save on milk. You won't eat dinner any more. You'll just meet at the dining table while you read out the recipes.

The bastard will re-marry with unseemly haste

Newly divorced men attract bimbos like flies to a dropped chop.

*

Even though he was conceived during the Aztec Empire he'll soon have a girlfriend so young that if she were a wine, you wouldn't drink her. Even Berlusconi wouldn't drink her.

*

If he leaves you for a younger woman with a pierced tongue,

remind him that a tongue stud weeping pus does not enhance fellatio. If she wanted to make a hole in her head, wouldn't it have been easier for all concerned if she'd used an AK47?

*

A good indication that your marriage really is over is when your husband proposes to someone else. You'll feel like the food on the supermarket shelf, with your obsolescence date-stamped on your forehead. You're little more than a brood mare put out to pasture.

*

You've only been divorced six weeks. Where did he get her? A *fiancée-vending machine?*

*

When your husband announces his engagement, you'll have to think of a congratulatory present. But what do you give the woman who's had everyone? Perhaps some genital lice to go with that syphilitic ulcer?

*

There's every chance that this time he'll pick a woman who introduces herself as an actress. Tell all your mutual friends that judging by the combination of cleavage and IQ, it's pretty clear she got her start in films entitled *Moist Choir Girl* and *Make Your Own Ben Wa Balls*. Her only ambition is to be a contestant on *Big Brother* – only she doesn't have the brains.

*

When your ex-husband actually sets a marriage date you will eventually wish him well . . . straight after you put his nuts through a garlic press. Meanwhile there are many things you can say to him to make yourself feel better. Tell him any of the following:

1) He'd be better off marrying a shopping trolley. At least it has a mind of its own.

2) 'So, when your new wife was filling in the consent form, where it said "sign" did she write Pisces or Aquarius?'

3) 'Why bother having a wedding lunch? She'll only throw it up again five minutes later.'

4) 'How could anyone get into such a tight pair of pants? I guess a glass of champagne usually does the trick.'

*

If you ever meet her, airheads will roll. But actually it's a mistake to think she's a bimbo. The woman's a praying mantis in Prada. Let's face it, it takes a lot of intelligence to look that stupid.

*

The only difference between a bimbo and a piranha is the silicone implant.

*

Yes, it's normal to feel a visceral revulsion to the idea of the man you once loved naked and ecstatic in the arms of a lower life form. But for the sake of your children, keep smiling. Smile until your gums dry out.

*

There's nothing worse than being left for a younger woman after you've ruined your body having his babies. But remind yourself that the man is evil. It's a wonder he's not off somewhere tossing virgins into volcanoes.

*

Pretend to wish them the best for their honeymoon, while all the time wishing that their plane makes unexpected contact with the Andes.

*

Take heart though. His new bride's so thin, if their plane *does* crash in the Andes there'll be nothing for him to eat.

Recovery from the husbandectomy

Don't dwell on the negative. You'll be thinking, I'm a divorcee with two children and no job. Who'll want me? I'll end up choking to death on people's leftovers in some tacky little eatery in King's Cross where nobody knows the Heimlich manoeuvre. But think of the positive things – no more snoring or boring. No more pretending to laugh at his inane anecdotes. You can now get an exotic pet, dye your hair fire-engine red and wear nothing but leopardskin. You'll soon feel more alive than cystitis-curing Greek yoghurt.

*

Your new motto: I think, therefore I'm divorced.

*

If you're honest, even if you did get a chance to reminisce with your hubby about all the fun times you shared, you'd be chatting for . . . oh, about 3.6 seconds.

*

In truth, that ex-husband of yours never exactly knocked himself out for you. Although it's tempting to bloody well do it for him.

*

Do you know why divorces are so expensive? Because they're worth it.

*

You will get over him. Soon you'll be about as nostalgic for your hubby as you are about those stitches in your perineum.

*

A divorced woman's motto? When it's raining shit, get a brolly.

*

Alternatively, you could just kill him . . .

*

Admirable restraint is what we dumped wives exercise right up to the moment when we shoot our marauding husbands.

*

Marriage is a fun-packed, frivolous hobby, only occasionally resulting in death.

CHAPTER 10

Murder — Till Homicide Do Us Part

People often ask, how can you tell if your marriage is truly dead? Well, I think a pretty good indication is if you're in a morgue identifying the body of your spouse.

*

Where there's a will, you should make sure you're in it . . .

*

Not all men are bastards – some of them are dead.

*

I find that a husband's opinion of his wife is greatly influenced by whether or not she is holding a gun to his head.

*

Apparently there *is* an afterlife; after your husband dies.

*

Is killing your husband an underhanded thing to do? Probably. But life teaches women a maths lesson not covered at school: when the odds are against you, get even.

*

Tell your hubby what a big day he has ahead of him. 'Tomorrow, I'm going to kill you, cut you into tiny pieces, then cash in your life insurance.'

*

But how to kill him? Can't live with him, can't cut him up with a chainsaw and dispose of his body in black bin-liners 'cause the neighbours might notice.

*

Sadly, the use of the hemlock-poisoned chalice seems to have died out in modern marriage.

*

If you walk into a garage to buy a can of petrol and the attendant asks you which brand your husband wants you to get, reply that your husband doesn't know yet that you are going to set fire to him. Run away while he's dialling the police.

*

The interesting thing about looking at a knife aimed at your ex-husband's groin is how small the tip of the blade is, and yet what a huge hole it would make in his future reproductive plans.

*

Now that you're single you're supposed to be mastering your own DIY, but your only pressing concern is which kitchen appliance can be used as a deadly weapon against your husband's lover – and the scene be made to look like an accident. Does the local hardware store sell a shallow grave shovel?

*

Every woman wants to be wanted – just not by the entire Metropolitan Police Force.

*

If you don't get a grip you're going to end up as one of those women on a confessional daytime telly show called *I Chopped Up My Husband's Lover and Fed Her to Him in a Lovely Tasty Casserole*.

*

You plan to kill him in a drive-by shooting . . . except your husband took the car. So what are you gonna do? A drive-by shooting *on a bus*?

*

The best way to a man's heart is through his stomach – with an upwards thrust from a carving knife.

*

These feelings are normal. After an acrimonious divorce, you'll have an overpowering urge to murder every man you've ever met – and your period's not due for ages.

PMS is justification for homicide. Just explain that you were going through your premenstrual-tension nervous breakdown Blue Period.

A wife's motto: I'm having my period so can therefore legally kill you.

But you'll have to *prove* you were premenstrual. I don't think they'll let you off for PPMS – Premature Premenstrual Syndrome. Or PMSHOFLM – Post-Menstrual Syndrome Hanging Over from Last Month.

*

If you kill him when you're postnatal, you can definitely get off. But don't leave it till the kid is one or two or you'll get a jail sentence. And you don't want a little baby in prison: the tooth fairy will have to commit a crime to leave the twenty pence under his pillow. His knowledge of primary colours will stop at grey . . . He'll be teething on steel bars. He won't be learning to read from *Spot Goes to the Circus* but graffiti along the lines of '*Die Police Scum*' . . . You want him to be able to count, sure, but not in lieu of knowing people's names. 'Will number 236 please pass me my bottle?'

Also, prison is such a grotty place. There'll be so much hair clogging the shower drain that you'll be tempted to get down and shampoo it. It'll be the only plughole you've ever seen which needs a cut and blow-dry. But bending over in the near vicinity of a male prison warder is a major misdemeanour. 'Bend Over; I'll Drive' is his motto. You'll spend all your waking hours watching male warders with what can only be described as mounting apprehension.

*

So on balance I think it best not to kill your hubby if you can possibly help it. Whatever you do to him might originally be reported as an accident, but not after those highly advanced forensic tests prove that his heart was gouged out of his body by his wife's nail file. Forget red-blooded murder and opt for revenge instead . . .

Revenge

Post divorce, you won't know whether to vent your spleen or rupture his.

You now have enough chips on his shoulder to open a casino.

You're probably pondering the Uzi machine-gun, hostage-taking and gradual-posting-of-bits-of-his-body-for-ransom option. That option looks quite attractive at this point but . . .

Don't get your tampon in a twist – just have revenge.

You could stalk him. The psychopath in the movie *Fatal Attraction* will have nothing on you . . . But that means you might be caught on closed-circuit security cameras *while having a bad hair day*. (Otherwise known as a 'Lockerbie' – a hair disaster.) It can be so traumatic finding a ladder in your stocking, once you've got one over your face.

*

Try more subtle techniques. They say revenge is a dish best served cold. Gazpacho is best served cold. Some tips for hot revenge:

1) Put Nair hair remover in his shampoo bottle.

2) Turn up his bathroom scales by half a stone – the best revenge on a weight-conscious egotist.

3) Drown him by putting a mirror on the bottom of his Jacuzzi.

4) Replace his KY Jelly with a tube of superglue – that will fix him. Literally.

5) The thought of a Rottweiler shag-o-gram should also cheer you up considerably.

6) Send him a gift voucher . . . for a castration.

7) Send an application to a computer dating agency in his name, citing his preference for geriatric, kinky amputees whose hobbies include penis-piercing.

8) Place a huge amplifier outside his bedroom window playing a Wings album at top volume. Or a Yoko Ono back-up vocal *on an isolated track*.

9) Encourage your 10-year-old to leave her descant recorder

at her father's place, so that she has something to play when she is staying over. Oh, and her violin too. The bagpipes are also an excellent instrument to take up. And do give the kids a little lecture on helping Dad to set the table. Forks on the left and. . . knives in the bimbo's back.

CHAPTER 11
Men
(some general tips)

The sex war

If only we didn't have such good taste in enemies.

*

But how can it be a battle of wits when he's unarmed?

*

Men are the reason God invented cake.

It's a man's world

Even God is a bloke. Why else do women suffer period cramps, pregnancy, childbirth, mastitis and the menopause? And then, just when everything goes quiet and you think it's all over, do you know what happens? *You grow a beard.* Is that fair, I ask you?

Usefulness

Now that women are economically independent and we can impregnate ourselves, if our vibrators could kill spiders in the bathroom, light the barbie and tell us we don't look fat in stretch Lycra, would we need men at all?

*

Men are as useful as a solar-powered vibrator on a rainy day.

Attitude

Men can never admit they are wrong. Women can admit they are wrong . . . starting with having chosen a guy who can't!

Weather

Men say that women are like cyclones: they're wet when they come and take the house when they go. Women know better – it's *men* who are like cyclones: you never know when they're coming, how long they'll stay . . . or how many inches you're gonna get.

Holidays . . .

Are like men too – never long enough.

Objects

Men don't treat women like objects. Hell, no. They treat their objects *way* better.

Socializing

Men always want to leave parties early. They're social premature ejaculators.

Brains

The reason men have that tiny hole in the end of their penises is so they can think with an open mind. A man's undies are always ruminating.

*

If you see a man idly scratching himself in the groin area, he's not itchy. He's just thinking.

Idolization

Never put a man on a pedestal. The only time a man should be put on a pedestal is when he's too short to change your light bulbs.

What men want

Basically, what all men want is a lingerie model with a tubal ligation, a Ph.D, and a private income.

Map reading

Let's call a truce on map-reading fights. I admit most women use a map-reading technique along the lines of 'It's one finger-nail's length further towards the red dot and then veer left.' Or 'Wales? Oh yes. Head for Harvey Nichols and turn right.'

But men refuse to admit they're lost even after you've spent what seems like an entire week on one seven-lane sub-orbital ring road and everyone in the car has started to resemble passengers on the raft of the *Medusa*.

Men would rather die than ask directions. Which is why they always include a woman in the space shuttle now.

Mind you, a woman's favourite destination is a cosy little spot which goes by the name of 'G'. Find *that* and she'll be really happy. That's one gadget men really do need – a TwatNav.

Cars

Men think 'sex drive' means doing it in the car – probably because of that little sign on the rear-view mirror which reads, 'Objects in this mirror may appear larger than they are.'

*

All men think they're good drivers. When he gets a note under his windscreen saying 'parking fine' he thinks it's a complimentary comment on his driving skills.

Sex appeal

The trouble with male sex appeal is that they give generously.

Misogyny

Misogynists make you rethink Darwin. They disprove the theory of evolution – they're evolving into apes.

Change

If a man ever tells you he can change, say, 'Hey, what's that noise? . . . Oh, it's the sound of millions of women laughing themselves to death.'

*

A woman thinks, OK, her man has a few flaws but with time she can change him . . . Men know that the only time they've ever been changed by a woman was out of their nappies as a baby.

*

Men changing? It won't ever happen. It's as likely as the washing-machine repair man turning up at the right time on the appointed day.

Ego

Calling men selfish is like calling a dwarf short.

*

The average man's ego is not just BIG. We're talking Visible from Outer Space. It'll be there on the satellite photos, along with the Great Wall of China and the Barrier bloody Reef.

Fidelity

Most men think monogamy is something you make dining-room tables out of.

*

Unless crossed, the female of the species tends towards fidelity and constancy. There are a few species where the male stays faithful until he dies, mostly as a result of being eaten by his partner after mating.

*

The only way most wives could ever have sex with a man other than her husband is to have a fantasy . . . Fantasize that *she's* someone else. Cameron Diaz, say, or Angelina Jolie.

Feelings

How can a man explain his feelings when he doesn't know he has them?

*

When it comes to emotions, men have a carp-like attention span. It's a kind of empathy amnesia. The only good thing is you can make cracks in front of men about how inadequate they are, because they're not listening anyway.

Communication

Like airbags in a car, sensitivity in a man is an optional extra.

*

Women spend more time thinking about what men are thinking about than men spend thinking.

*

Maybe your husband doesn't have the best emotional responses, compared to other men, or even certain species of plankton. But he's not alone. Most husbands are inattentive. You could leave them at the beginning of the football season and they wouldn't notice till the end.

*

For women, wordplay is foreplay. How else is Woody Allen still getting laid? Women love a little punnilingus.

*

You're better off engaging in a heated argument with your pillow over whether or not you're having a supportive relationship.

*

The only interest the average man has in 'personal growth' is his morning erection.

*

If your husband says there's nothing to talk about, tell him that yes there is. Your impending divorce.

Midlife crisis

A few years into the marriage and his mind starts wandering – a shame, as it really is too small to be allowed out on its own.

*

When friends ask, 'Where is your husband?' reply, 'Attending the birth of his next wife, probably.'

Pets

The reason I hate animals is because I went out with so many as a teenager.

*

Don't consider getting a pet until your husband has learned to come to heel when called.

*

I have accidentally discovered a home-grown solution to getting rid of laughter lines. Have a male partner who collects snakes and, believe me, you will never laugh, smile or vaguely relax ever, ever again. Especially when the mouse he buys to feed it escapes. The *pregnant* mouse. Nothing like roaming your own home with a net and a tranquillizer dart to take the joy out of life.

Hypochondria

'Hypochondria' is Greek for 'man'. If a man denies this, then hypochondria is the only disease he doesn't have. Men just can't leave being well enough alone. 'So you really think I'm a hypochondriac?' he'll ask in a worried voice. He'll then get hypochondriacal about being a hypochondriac. His ailments will soon be killing you! One measly headache and it's a swelling brainstem, one pee too often and it's prostate cancer . . . You'll start to forget what he looks like without a thermometer wedged between his teeth.

*

A man's wedding vows should be 'In sickness and in sickness, I now pronounce you . . .'

*

Women get colds, headaches, the blues . . . Men with exactly the same symptoms get the flu, a migraine and a midlife crisis. Women on the other hand are *psychological* hypochondriacs. We take our emotional temperature all day. Am I happy? Could I be happier? Is he really the right man for me?

Ask these questions too often and it will be time you took the temperature of your relationship with a *rectal* thermometer.

*

Nobody ever said marriage was going to be easy. In sickness and in health and all that . . . and believe me, if you marry into allergies like I did, there's always going to be a little something wrong.

*

Simply tell him they've finally found a cure for hypochondria – death.

Sport

Men can play golf all day and tell you that it's business. Why can't women do the same thing with clothes buying? 'I'll be dress shopping for eight hours with the girls. I don't want to go but, you know, it's for the *business*.'

Sport is nothing more than housework avoidance. The football season and the cricket last for months. Why can't women have a shoe-shopping season? 'It's shoe-shopping season, dear. I'll see you in February.'

*

Don't let him talk you into competing in a marathon. A 'fun run' is a contradiction in terms.

Cricket

I have had marriages that have lasted less time than a test match. It's Wagner – with wickets. The sport version of tantric sex – but the only thing which gets sticky is the wicket.

Toilet training

If men are so superior at spatial awareness why do they always pee on the bathroom floor? (Try painting a bullseye in the loo bowl.)

*

Men think that sitting on the toilet is a leisure activity.

*

In a woman's equivalent 'leisure' time she will wrap the schoolbooks in plastic, write the Christmas cards, paste holiday snaps into photo albums, pack the dishwasher, unpack the dishwasher, alphabetize the condiments cupboard, make the kids' lunches, press the kids' uniforms, shine the kids' school shoes, sort out the money for the school excursions, finish the kids' homework (which involves reading all of *Ulysses* in Greek), take the dog for a walk because nobody else will, get masochistically waxed for her man, hand-bake the Swedish muesli because one of the kids has gone vegetarian, ring her mother-in-law to let her know how much her son loves her, attempt to master *coq au vin* for a dinner party for her husband's clients at short notice, finish off her own work from the office, catch the lost guinea pig which had vanished behind the bookshelf and spend half an hour looking for her man – who is still on the loo.

Camping

One of life's great mysteries is why people are divided into those who like the outdoors and those who like the indoors, and why they invariably end up married to each other.

Women are not that bonkers about the great bloody outdoors with all its multi-footed insects. We only like getting bitten all over by eligible blokes . . . But unfortunately the best place to find eligible blokes is in the great bloody outdoors. While a woman's natural habitat is an art gallery or concert hall, she'll invariably fall for the type of man who likes to toss a tent casually into his back pocket and disappear, at a jog, up Everest for a week or two.

*

While he enthuses about sleeping rough, living off the land, reading by candlelight and eating by the fireside . . . you'll feel he's just described fleeing the Taliban over the mountains of Afghanistan.

*

The trouble with camping is that life is not like *Winnie the Pooh*. Real animals don't want to befriend you; they want to *eat* you, instantly.

*

Men love to sleep under the stars. But 'sleep' is too optimistic a word. It's impossible to get any rest. Mainly because some insect is always blinking its 9,000,624,439,002 eyes at you in the dark.

*

Most men want to get back to nature. Most women want to get back at nature or to the nearest luxury hotel suite.

Beauty versus brains

Why do men prefer beauty to brains? Because they see better than they think.

*

Women suffer from facial prejudice. We get judged on our looks in a way that men don't.

*

Up against a sex goddess, principles and profundity are about as useful as a eunuch at a whipped-cream orgy.

*

Opera's the only place in the world where the fat chick gets laid.

*

Any girl can be alluring – all you have to do is stand still and look brain-dead.

*

A man can be so ugly it's a wonder he isn't in a bottle somewhere in a science lab, yet he feels free to judge a woman on her looks. Is there anything quite so annoying as having your physical shortcomings criticized by a man who should be imprisoned for persistent chest hair exposure? A man who is so Olympic Games ugly, you've seen better heads on a beer? Imagine if we judged men the same way – 'Sorry. No pecs, no sex.'

*

Cosmetic surgeons stand for whatever the general public will fall for. So don't give in to male 'shapists'. Just remember that . . .

Botox is what Saddam Hussein used to kill Kurds. You'll have a body more preserved than Lenin's. Why should women avoid all lines except Cunard?

Child-bearing lips   To achieve the look of having a giant vagina sutured to your face, you simply take the fat out of your bottom and inject it into your lips, so you're literally talking out of your arse. (It explains a *lot* about Hollywood.)

Liposuction   Having your bottom sliced off to please a man gives a new definition to 'lobotomy'.

What will you do with all the fat sucked out? Maybe you could have it sculpted into a statuette? Maybe that explains the Blob? It's escaped liposuctioned fat, running free.

Facelifts   Women only get a new face in the hope that a man will sit on it.

*

Beauty is a case of mind over matter – if you don't mind, it don't matter.

*

Spas are not so much about getting in touch with your inner you as getting in touch with your outer bank manager. Why bother buying the products and having the treatments? You might as well just record the sound of a cash register opening and closing. If the facially prejudiced man in your life tries to tell you that it's not so expensive, say, 'Yeah, you're right. No more expensive than, say, *maintaining a space programme.*'

*

There's only one way to get rid of unsightly fat. Divorce your couch potato husband.

*

Or get older friends. John Mortimer, my best friend, died at eighty-five. He thought I was a nymphette. He called himself my toyboy . . . although he added that it would take him three weeks to get a 'soft-on'.

*

Despite all that frantic hair-dyeing, the very best thing about us is grey: the substance between our ears. That is the only unique part of our bodies.

*

If a bloke is rude about your wrinkles or weight, tell him that they've found a cure for baldness. You know – *hair*.

Bald men

Men worry about baldness much more than we do. If he's all

angst-ridden, reassure him that he's not balding, he's just gaining more face.

*

If he's challenged at a follicular level, tell him that the men with acres of unkempt foliage on their craniums are much worse. Like Russell Brand. That's not hair. It's a lawn. That hair could have garden gnomes in it.

Fashion

Mutton   How often have you met a man whose aftershave is set to Stun, his trousers so tight ('grape-smugglers') that you can detect his religion? All this negativity about mutton dressed as lamb, what about mutton dressed as ram?

Advice   How to let a man know, subtly, that he has no fashion sense? Try , 'Well, it's a look. For a wino, maybe.' Or 'The only people who'll follow you in *those* clothes are store detectives.'

*

If your husband has really bad fashion sense but won't change, just seat him next to Germans. The best thing about Germans is that they'll be even more badly dressed than he is.

*

Men think it's logical to dress badly so that a woman will want nothing more than to get him out of those annoying clothes. 'You know what would look good on me?' a man is thinking. *You.*

Money belts

Wearing a bulging money belt at groin level is the male version of the Wonderbra. He's compensating for physical inadequacies.

Testicles

Too tight jeans mean his testicles have applied for a transfer.

Grooming

Life is so unfair. While we're toning and tanning and tweezing, all a man requires of his skin is that it grows hair and, when shaved, stops bleeding before he gets to the office.

Body hair

I have been out with men who are so hairy they require *nostril* mousse. What's foreplay for men like this? Combing bugs out of his back hair? He's not a man. He's a yeti. And yet he expects you to undergo a torturous Brazilian wax.

I like a bikini line in which you could stalk stags. Just convince him that he might discover the legendary lost temple of the Xingothuan tribe down there, or maybe a couple of *Big Brother* contestants who don't yet know the series is over. That will really excite him. While perhaps it's best not to have nipple hair you could weave into macramé hanging baskets, or a bikini line which could be gainfully trained up the side of a house – body hair is natural.

I like my pubic hair. It's like having a little pet in my pants. It's amazing my pudenda haven't been awarded National Park status. If I did take to my pubes with a pair of scissors, I'd be shouting 'Timber!' But then your vulva just looks ragged. Soon the general effect is of a moulting shag rug. Frantic, you keep on trimming and shaping until your spiky groin resembles a sea creature disturbed in a rock pool and preparing to attack. It gives 'bad hair day' a whole new meaning. Your pubic hairs could now shred a man, like Parmesan on a cheese grater. Your pudenda look like AstroTurf. You could play mini-golf down there. I never thought I'd be saying this but Bring Back Bush!

*

The reason blondes have more fun is because brunettes are too busy waxing, shaving, lasering and Nair hair removing for some man. But any woman who's wrestled with a DIY bikini-wax kit will never be quite the woman she once was.

Men and breasts

A male obsession with big breasts is possibly because he was bottle-fed as a baby. If your breasts are small, you try not to fret – but find yourself ordering a D cup of coffee at the café.

But if they're too big, men drool and slobber all over your boobs, as though they've forgotten you're there. Just say to him, 'Hey! Excuse me. When the three of you are through . . . lemme know, OK?'

*

But don't join the jut-set. Silicone breasts are like TV evangelists. You know they're fake but you can't stop looking at them. Jordan's boobs are so huge it would be more appropriate to say that her chest has had a *Jordan* implant. Pamela Anderson's breasts could be mistaken for a breakaway republic. And yet some men are more excited by breast implants than by the births of their babies. He'll take out an ad – 'I would like to announce the birth of a new chest. Mother and boobies doing well.'

*

£4,300 is the average cost of implants. What the hell are they made of? Caviar?

*

If you succumb to implants to please some man, the embarrassing thing is everybody knows they're fake. What can you say? 'These are not my real breasts. I'm just breaking them in for a friend.'

*

I once witnessed a breast implant operation. It was like an airline passenger trying to shove an inappropriate object into an overhead baggage compartment.

*

If a big-breasted woman draws attention to herself by announcing that she's saving up for a breast reduction, just reply, sweetly, 'Why? Isn't two the normal number?'

*

Never get breast surgery to please some bloke. A Wonderbra will do. (So called because when you take it off, you wonder where the hell your tits went.) Or just find a man who understands that more than a mouthful is a waste.

*

The good thing about small breasts is that people can always read the entire message on your T-shirts and you never have to wonder why you got the job.

Faults

Women have many faults. Men have only two. Everything they say, and everything they do.

*

If any man says he hasn't any faults, point out that that *is* a fault, actually – thinking you don't have any. A man who admits he's flawed is pretty much perfect in our eyes.

*

Because . . . do you know what women really want? A man who is perfect enough to understand why we're not.

Happy hunting.